Gudrun Schwarzer and Helmut Leder
(Editors)

The Development of Face Processing

Hogrefe & Huber

Library of Congress Cataloging-in-Publication Data

is now available via the Library of Congress Marc Database under the

LC Control Number: 2003104140

National Library of Canada Cataloguing-in-Publication Data

Schwarzer, Gudrun
    The development of face processing / Gudrun Schwarzer, Helmut Leder.

Includes bibliographical references.
ISBN 0-88937-264-0

    1. Face perception. I. Leder, Helmut II. Title.

BF242.S37 2003   153.7'5   C2003-901952-7

PUBLISHING OFFICES
USA: Hogrefe & Huber Publishers, 44 Brattle Street, 4th Floor,
             Cambridge, MA 02138
             Phone (866) 823-4726, Fax (617) 354-6875, E-mail info@hhpub.com
Europe: Hogrefe & Huber Publishers, Rohnsweg 25, D-37085 Göttingen, Germany,
             Phone +49 551 49609-0, Fax +49 551 49609-88, E-mail hh@hhpub.com

SALES & DISTRIBUTION
USA: Hogrefe & Huber Publishers, Customer Services Department,
             30 Amberwood Parkway, Ashland, OH 44805,
             Phone (800) 228-3749, Fax (419) 281-6883, E-mail custserv@hhpub.com
Europe: Hogrefe & Huber Publishers, Rohnsweg 25, D-37085 Göttingen, Germany,
             Phone +49 551 49609-0, Fax +49 551 49609-88, E-mail hh@hhpub.com

OTHER OFFICES
Canada: Hogrefe & Huber Publishers, 12 Bruce Park Avenue, Toronto, Ontario M4P 2S3
Switzerland: Hogrefe & Huber Publishers, Länggass-Strasse 76, CH-3000 Bern 9

Hogrefe & Huber Publishers
Incorporated and registered in the State of Washington, USA, and in Göttingen, Lower Saxony, Germany

Printed and bound in Germany
ISBN 0-88937-264-0

Table of Contents

Part I: Visual Cognitive Abilities in Infancy

1   Development of Fragmented Versus Holistic Object Perception
Scott P. Johnson

2   Infants' Preference for Texture-Defined Targets of Different Saliency: Evidence for Local Processing
Ruxandra Sireteanu, Irmgard Encke, and Iris Bachert

3   Development of Depth and Object Perception in Infancy
Michael Kavšek

Part II: Face Processing from Infancy to Adulthood

4   Face Processing During the First Decade of Life
Gudrun Schwarzer, Nicola Zauner, and Monika Korell

5   Development of Face Processing in Early Adolescence
Helmut Leder, Gudrun Schwarzer, and Steve Langton

6   Expert Face Processing: Specialization and Constraints
Adrian Schwaninger, Claus-Christian Carbon, and Helmut Leder

Part III: Applied Research on Face Processing in the Course of Development

7   A Framework for the Study and Treatment of Face Processing Deficits in Autism
James W. Tanaka, Samantha Lincoln, and Logan Hegg

8   Face Processing and Person Processing: Are They Both the Same?
Katja Seitz

9   Remembering Faces in Social Contexts
Claudia M. Roebers

Contributors

Iris Bachert
Department of Neurophysiology
Max Planck Institute for Brain Research
Deutschordenstr. 46
D-60528 Frankfurt/M.
Germany
E-mail: bachert@mpih-frankfurt.mpg.de

Claus-Christian Carbon
Department of Psychology
Free University of Berlin
Habelschwerdter Allee 45
D-14195 Berlin
Germany
E-mail: ccc@experimental-psychology.de

Irmgard Encke
Department of Neurophysiology
Max Planck Institute for Brain Research
Deutschordenstr. 46
D-60528 Frankfurt/M.
Germany

Logan Hegg
Department of Psychology
Severance Lab
Oberlin College
Oberlin, OH 44074
USA
E-mail: logan.hegg@oberlin.edu

Scott P. Johnson
Department of Psychology
Uris Hall
Cornell University
Ithaca, NY 14853
USA
E-mail: sj75@cornell.edu

Michael Kavšek
University of Bonn
Department of Psychology
Römerstr. 164
D-53117 Bonn
Germany
E-mail: kavsek@uni-bonn.de

Monika Korell
Friedrich-Miescher-Laboratory of the
Max Planck Society
Spemannstr. 34
D-72076 Tübingen
Germany
E-mail: monika.korell@tuebingen.mpg.de

Steve Langton
Department of Psychology
University of Stirling
FK9 4LA Stirling
Scotland
E-mail: srhl1@stirling.ac.uk

Helmut Leder
Department of Psychology
Free University of Berlin
Habelschwerdter Allee 45
D-14195 Berlin
Germany
E-mail: leder@experimental-psychology.de

Samantha Lincoln
Department of Psychology
Severance Lab
Oberlin College
Oberlin, OH 44074
USA
E-mail: samantha.lincoln@oberlin.edu

Claudia M. Roebers
University of Würzburg
Department of Psychology IV
Röntgenring 10
D-97070 Würzburg
Germany
E-mail: roebers@psychologie.uni-
wuerzburg.de

Adrian Schwaninger
Max Planck Institute for Biological
Cybernetics
Spemannstr. 38
D-72076 Tübingen
Germany
E-mail: adrian.schwaninger@tuebingen.mpg.de

Gudrun Schwarzer
Friedrich-Miescher-Laboratory of the
Max Planck Society
Spemannstr. 34
D-72076 Tübingen
Germany
E-mail: gudrun.schwarzer@tuebingen.mpg.de

Katja Seitz
Catholic University of Eichstätt-Ingolstadt
Department of Psychology
Ostenstr. 26-28
D-85072 Eichstätt
Germany
E-mail: katja.seitz@ku-eichstaett.de

Ruxandra Sireteanu
Department of Biological Psychology
Institute for Psychology
Johann Wolfgang Goethe-University Frankfurt
Mertonstr. 17
D-60054 Frankfurt/M.
Germany
and
Department of Neurophysiology
Max Planck Institute for Brain Research
Deutschordenstr. 46
D-60528 Frankfurt/M.
Germany
E-mail: sireteanu@mpih-frankfurt.mpg.de

James W. Tanaka
Department of Psychology
Severance Lab
Oberlin College
Oberlin, OH 44074
USA
E-mail: tanaka@cs.oberlin.edu

Nicola Zauner
Friedrich-Miescher-Laboratory of the
Max Planck Society
Spemannstr. 34
D-72076 Tübingen
Germany
E-mail: nicola.zauner@tuebingen.mpg.de

Foreword

Interest in how faces are perceived and recognized has captured the imagination of philosophers and scientists for well over a century. Nowhere has this interest been more enthusiastic and long-lived than in the broad discipline of psychology. For example, cognitive psychologists and neuroscientists are interested in faces as they may represent a prototype of a stimulus that has been accorded special status by the brain. Evolutionary psychologists are interested in face recognition because it appears to be a "special" ability that has been selected for through evolutionary pressures and conserved across species. Finally, developmental psychologists have long been interested in face recognition because faces provide an early channel of communication (prior to the onset of language) between infant and caregiver. Moreover, because the ability to recognize faces occurs so early in the life span, it may represent a model system for teasing apart experiential vs. non-experiential contributions to a specific perceptual-cognitive system.

The chapters that comprise this book focus on two very fundamental questions: What factors are driving the development of face recognition from infancy through adulthood, and what processes underlie the continued elaboration and refinement of this ability through adulthood? These topics are addressed from a variety of perspectives that collectively sum to an excellent tutorial on the ontogeny and development of face processing. Given the continued interest in this skill by cognitive psychologists, and the newly established interest in face processing by developmental cognitive neuroscientists, this book could not be timelier.

Charles A. Nelson
University of Minnesota

Preface

The chapters in the present volume were originally papers presented at the international workshop on "The Development of Face Processing" at the Friedrich-Miescher-Laboratory of the Max Planck Society in Tübingen, Germany. For the first time, researchers on the development of face processing and visual processing in general came together and presented and discussed their work in a productive environment. We would like to acknowledge the support for our work on this volume from the German Research Foundation and the Max Planck Society.

Over the past 10 years, there has been a growing interest in understanding face processing. One reason for this growth in interest may be that faces are very special. The human ability to differentiate among extremely large sets of faces and to recall specific faces is exceptional. Faces provide the main means of recognizing others and of communicating with others about feelings, moods, and intentions, thus lending faces a particularly important social function. For a couple of years, it has now been possible to study face processing by using methods that are widely accepted by experimental psychology.

One of the most fundamental questions in the field of face processing is: What are the roots of and what are the reasons for our impressive ability to process faces? How much is this ability innate and what do we learn as we develop? Understanding the ontogenetic origin of face processing as well as the processes that are responsible for age-specific changes in face processing will also provide important information on the nature of adults' face processing. Interestingly, children and adults are equally fascinated by faces, and parents often spend considerable time in close facial contact with their babies wondering how much the babies understand of their visual surroundings. Also, as adults believe faces to be very special, we expect faces to be of special significance to babies too.

So far, previous research on the development of face processing can be characterized by three observations: (1) It mainly focuses on face perception in newborns and young infants. (2) There is very little knowledge available about developmental changes in the period between infancy and young adulthood. (3) Most importantly, research on the development of face processing is virtually unconnected to visual-perceptual development in general. The present volume extends the current state of research on all three of these points. Moreover, it connects studies on face processing in infancy with studies concerning the development of face processing and it builds a bridge between studies on face processing and studies on visual perceptual development. Researchers from the US as well as from Europe who have conducted pioneering work in these research areas and who anticipate future interest in this domain are contributors to this book.

The present volume consists of 3 sections which include 9 chapters. In the first three chapters Scott P. Johnson (Cornell University, Ithaca), Ruxandra Sireteanu, Irmgard Encke, and Iris Bachert (Max Planck Institute of Brain Science, Frankfurt/M.), and Michael Kavšek (University of Bonn) describe and explain fundamental visual cognitive abilities in infancy. Scott P. Johnson's chapter focuses on the question of how and when infants process whole objects across space and time when occluded objects are presented. Ruxandra Sireteanu, Irmgard Encke, and Iris Bachert explain how infants segment and bind features to perceive homogeneous stimuli. The third chapter written by Michael Kavšek is concerned with the question of whether and if so, when infants are able to use depth and form cues to perceive objects. In sum, the three chapters give an overview over infants' visual abilities that should be considered when face perception in infancy is examined.

The subsequent three chapters focus on research concerning the development of face processing. Gudrun Schwarzer, Nicola Zauner, and Monika Korell (Friedrich-Miescher-Laboratory of the Max Planck Society) describe face processing in infancy and subsequent development until the age of 10 years, concentrating mainly on the question of whether infants and older children process faces by orientating towards single facial features (analytic processing) or by orientating towards overall similarity of faces (holistic processing). In the next chapter, Helmut Leder (Free University of Berlin), Gudrun Schwarzer, and Steve Langton (University of Stirling) provide an overview of the development of face processing in 10-year-olds to 16-year-olds. The last chapter of this section focus on face processing in adults. Here Adrian Schwaninger (Max Planck Institute for Biological Cybernetics), Claus-Christian Carbon (Free University of Berlin), and Helmut Leder describe effects of expertise in adults' face recognition.

The third section of the book is concerned with applied research of the development of face processing. James W. Tanaka, Samantha Lincoln, and Logan Hegg (Oberlin College) elucidate a framework for the study and treatment of face processing deficits in autistic children. The subsequent two chapters study the development of face processing in social contexts. Katja Seitz (University of Eichstätt-Ingolstadt) describes to what extent findings concerning the development of face processing can be transferred to the development of processing individual people. Claudia M. Roebers (University of Würzburg) investigates processes of face recognition in neutral, experimental contexts compared to social contexts such as the context of testimony.

Together, the chapters of the present book provide a reasonable foundation for understanding the changes in face processing during development but also stress where further research should be carried out to increase our knowledge in this area.

Gudrun Schwarzer and Helmut Leder

Part I:
Visual Cognitive Abilities in Infancy

Development of Fragmented Versus Holistic Object Perception

Scott P. Johnson

1.1 Introduction

Our environment is filled with objects at various distances, many of which are partly occluded by other objects that are closer to the observer. Our *visual* environment, that is, what we experience as we look around us, does not match the physical environment, because it consists of fragments of object surfaces, a set of colored and textured shapes that shifts with every change in eye or head position. Yet we do not experience our surroundings as fragmented, but instead we perceive it accurately, as composed of objects that are only partly revealed. The mature visual system, therefore, is adept at going beyond the information that is directly available, in imparting our everyday experience of the objects in our surroundings as coherent and unified across space and time, and with continual changes in viewpoint. This chapter will articulate a program of research that probes developmental origins of this perceptual skill in humans.

To anticipate, I will describe experiments that provide evidence that infants are born with a functional visual system that is sufficient to achieve many kinds of perceptual discrimination. Nevertheless, neonates do not appear capable of perceiving occlusion. Neonates' object perception, then, is *fragmented*, because they are limited to detecting only the surfaces of objects that are directly visible, and fail to perceive objects as continuous beyond the point of occlusion. The progression toward *holistic* object perception occurs over the next several months, with the ability to integrate surface fragments over increasing spatial distance and, in the case of objects that go fully out of sight, over increasing temporal durations.

In addition to studies that examine the change from fragmented to holistic object perception, I will describe additional experiments that have investigated more closely the visual cues used by infants to accomplish perception of unified objects under occlusion. These experiments have revealed that by 4 months of age, infants are sensitive to and utilize a range of visual information in these tasks, including surface motion and orientation. The chapter will conclude with a consideration of possible mechanisms of development.

1.2 Development of Perception of Object Unity

1.2.1 History

Investigations of infants' responses to objects under occlusion have their roots in observations by Piaget (1952) concerning manual search behavior of infants when confronted with a situation in which a desired toy was covered by a blanket. Prior to 8 months, infants would not search for the toy under these circumstances, even though they were capable of the individual actions necessary for toy retrieval (lifting the blanket and grasping the toy). Starting at about 6 months, however, infants would recover the toy when it was only *partly* hidden, a behavior Piaget termed "reconstruction of an invisible whole from a visible fraction." This behavior, and others, were incorporated into Piaget's account of development of object permanence: the knowledge of an object as existing independently of an infant's perceptual contact.

Bower (1967) examined more closely the nature of this kind of reconstruction with a task in which 1-month-old infants viewed a triangle made of wire, its center occluded by a rectangular object (see Figure 1).

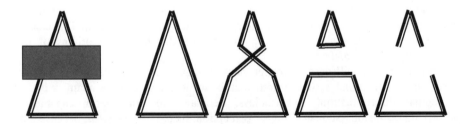

Figure 1. Training (left) and four test stimuli used in the Bower (1967) experiment on 1-month-olds' perception of a partly occluded wire triangle.

Bower used an operant sucking procedure and reasoned that reduced sucking rates upon presentation of a novel stimulus would indicate perceptual discrimination of the new stimulus from the original. The infants viewed four test stimuli (presented individually), a complete triangle, a triangle with crossed lines at the previous place of intersection, an incomplete triangle, and a small triangle paired with a quadrilateral. All four test stimuli were consistent with the visible portions of the partly occluded figure seen during training, but the infants maintained sucking rates to the complete object and reduced sucking rates most in response to the two incomplete forms. This implies generalization of the complete form to the partly occluded object, and response to the incomplete forms as novel.

Kellman and Spelke (1983) noted the inconsistencies evident in the observations by Piaget (1952) and Bower (1967) and undertook a more thorough examination of conditions under which young infants would perceive partly occluded objects. They developed a procedure based on visual habituation and response recovery that has become a standard method in this type of investigation. Infants were first presented with a partly occluded rod until looking times declined according to a predetermined criterion. The infants then viewed complete and broken versions of the rod (see Figure 2). The test stimulus that attracted the most attention was assumed to be perceived as most novel relative to the initial stimulus, on the logic that infants exhibit novelty preferences following habituation (Bornstein, 1985). Kellman and Spelke reported that 4-month-old infants showed reliable preferences for a broken rod test display when the partly occluded rod (the habituation stimulus) was seen to move laterally relative to the background and occluder (as depicted in Figure 2). (Control experiments ruled out the likelihood of other potential explanations for this result, such as an inherent preference for the broken object.) There was no evidence of unity perception, however, in displays in which the rod remained stationary, in contradiction to the results reported by Bower.

Two conclusions were drawn from this work (Kellman & Spelke, 1983). First, perception of partly occluded objects was proposed to stem from an innate (i.e., unlearned) conception of objects as continuous and persistent under occlusion. Second, the principal source of information specifying unity for infants was common motion. Alignment of edges across the occluder was proposed to have little contribution to the effect. The question of development of unity perception across infancy will be discussed in the rest of this section; the question of visual cues that specify unity will be discussed in the following section.

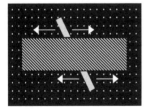 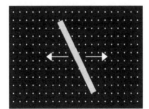 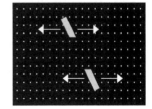

Figure 2. Stimuli used to test perception of object unity using a visual habituation paradigm. Adapted from Johnson and Aslin (1996).

1.2.2 Development

1.2.2.1 Neonates' Perception of Object Unity

The claim that unity perception is innate was tested in a series of experiments by Slater and colleagues (Slater, Johnson, Brown, & Badenoch, 1996; Slater, Morison, Somers, Mattock, Brown, & Taylor, 1990). Following the methods devised by Kellman and Spelke (1983), they found a consistent preference by neonates for a complete object subsequent to habituation to a partly occluded object, indicating that neonates do not perceive unity, but instead appear to detect only the visible portions in these displays. A series of control conditions mitigated against the possibility that other factors were responsible for these findings, such as a familiarity preference (rather than a novelty preference). These experiments do not support the contention that perception of object unity is available innately, and raise the question of the time course of development across the first several months after birth.

1.2.2.2 Developmental Changes in Unity Perception

The question of development of perception of object unity has been explored in detail by Johnson and colleagues. In the first of these investigations, we tested 2-month-olds' unity perception in rod-and-box displays, and found no reliable posthabituation preference (Johnson & Náñez, 1995). In contrast, a group of 4-month-olds whom we observed looked longer at the broken rod (replicating the Kellman & Spelke, 1983 result). These findings suggest that unity perception emerges rather gradually across the first four months.

In a follow-up investigation, we questioned this interpretation by presenting 2-month-olds displays in which information for unity was enhanced by reducing the occluder, such that more of the occluded rod was visible (e.g., by using a box reduced in height; Johnson & Aslin, 1995). In these experiments, the 2-month-olds showed a strong and consistent preference for the broken rod following habituation. This result narrows the age range of development to only 2 months after birth, implying that the shift toward the ability to perceive object unity is a very rapid developmental phenomenon. However, these experiments do not inform the more important question of how it is that infants come to perceive unity after an initial failure to do so, a question that is addressed in the final section of this chapter.

1.3 Infants' Sensitivity to Visual Information Specifying Unity

The object unity paradigm has been used extensively to probe the specific kinds of visual information that infants and adults utilize to make perceptual judgments about unity. These investigations have tended to focus on three cues: motion and orientation of edges on either side of the occluder, and depth cues. Each is addressed in turn.

1.3.1 Motion and Other Kinds of Synchronous Change

The role of motion in unity perception has been explored by manipulating which surfaces are made to move in partial occlusion displays, and the kinds of motion and other synchronous change over time that the surfaces undergo.

1.3.1.1 Which Surfaces Move is Important

Kellman and Spelke (1983) varied systematically the motion of rod and occluder in several experiments: the rod parts moving relative to a stationary occluder (described previously), the occluder moving relative to a stationary rod, the rod parts and occluder undergoing a common motion, and finally, all display elements stationary (also described previously). Only in the first condition did infants provide evidence of unity perception. It appears, therefore, that there is more to the role of motion than simply providing information for the separation of the stimulus components from each other and from the background: It seems more likely that motion enters more directly into the unity process. Precisely how this happens, however, remains unknown.

1.3.1.2 How Surfaces Move is Important

1.3.1.2.1 Horizontal Motion, Vertical Motion, and Motion in Depth

Kellman, Spelke, and Short (1986) employed rod-and-box displays similar to those described by Kellman and Spelke (1983), who had presented rod parts undergoing horizontal translation in the frontal plane. Kellman et al., however, used vertical motion of the rod, relative to a stationary occluder, as well as motion in depth (toward and away from the infant as she viewed the display during habituation). Broken and complete rod test displays moved in the same manner as the rod parts during habituation. In both of these conditions, the infants appeared to perceive unity, suggesting that the kind of motion is less important than the mere fact of motion in specifying unity.

1.3.1.2.2 Rotation and Oscillation

Eizenman and Bertenthal (1998) investigated the possibility that object rotation would support infants' unity perception by presenting 4- and 6-month-olds with a partly occluded rod undergoing either rotation in the frontal plane through 360° (like a propeller), or oscillatory (back-and-forth) motion through 90°. The younger infants provided no evidence of unity perception in either display. The older infants perceived unity only when the occluder was circular, and the appearance of the rod remained constant across rotation (i.e., the visible portions did not shorten and lengthen as the rod rotated).

Johnson, Cohen, Marks, and Johnson (in press) noted that frontal rotation might present a special challenge to unity perception: It might be especially difficult to integrate the upper and lower visible rod portions, which are moving in opposite directions on either side of the occluder, into a percept of coherent motion. We presented a partly occluded wedge shape (i.e., akin to a doorstop) undergoing vertical rotation (around the object's center axis) to 2- and 4-month-olds, and found evidence of robust perception of unity under these conditions. Rotation, therefore, can be an important source of information for young infants' perception of object unity and shape.

1.3.1.3 Other Kinds of Synchronous Change

Motion is only one part of a larger class of visual cues that provides information for change over time. Jusczyk, Johnson, Spelke, and Kennedy (1999) examined other kinds of synchronous temporal change, including cyclic changes in color and luminance of rod parts above and below an occluding box. We varied several aspects of these kinds of change (e.g., colors and flash rates) and found that infants were unable to use any of the non-motion synchronous changes we employed to perceive unity.

Taken together, therefore, experiments that examine motion and other types of change with time reveal that motion seems to have a special status to young infants' object perception. It is important to note, however, that in all of the experiments described in this section of the chapter, displays were used that presented *surface* motion – that is, there is a set of visible surfaces that move or otherwise change in synchrony. As a result of this work, we know the importance of temporal relations between surfaces that contribute to perceptual integration.

But what of the *spatial* relations between the surfaces? Recall the second conclusion drawn by Kellman and Spelke (1983) regarding infants' perception of object unity: Alignment of edges across the occluder does not influence the effect. The next section of the chapter examines this conclusion.

1.3.2 Edge and Surface Configuration

My colleagues and I have undertaken an extensive series of investigations to explore the role of edge orientation and other issues of surface configuration in infants' perception of object unity.

1.3.2.1 Edge Alignment

In the experiments described previously, the objects used in tests for unity perception had edges that were aligned across the occluder. Only when the edges moved together did infants provide evidence of unit formation; there was no evidence of perception of unity perception of aligned, static edges. Kellman (1993) proposed that sensitivity to alignment as a cue for unity follows a two-step process. Initially, infants were thought to rely on motion information only in determining whether edges were unified. Some time later (perhaps around 6 months), infants used configural information as well, such as alignment.

Johnson and Aslin (1996) tested this hypothesis by habituating 4-month-old infants to rod-and-box displays in which rod segments were oriented such that they would either meet behind the occluder if extended, the *misaligned rod* display (Figure 3, left), or would not meet, the *nonaligned rod* display (Figure 3, right). In both instances, the rod parts underwent a common lateral motion. The infants then viewed broken and complete versions of the stimuli, following the methods described previously. If the Kellman (1993) hypothesis were correct, we would expect to find unity perception in both displays, but a very different pattern resulted. The infants responded to the misaligned rod display as if unity (or its opposite, a percept of disjoint objects) were indeterminate, and responded to the nonaligned rod display as if it were composed of disjoint objects. This provides evidence against the thesis that young infants are insensitive to edge configuration as information feeding into the process of unity perception. It is important to point out, nevertheless, that alignment without motion is insufficient to support unity percepts in 4-month-olds (Kellman & Spelke, 1983; Jusczyk et al., 1999).

1.3.2.2 Surface Configuration

The Johnson and Aslin (1996) finding of edge sensitivity in 4-month-olds leads to the prediction that motion is insufficient to specify unity in the absence of aligned edges (i.e., the converse of the Kellman, 1993 hypothesis). Johnson, Bremner, Slater, and Mason (2000) tested this prediction with displays in which partly occluded objects moved back and forth. They were arranged such that at the points of intersection of object and occluder, there were no aligned edges, but the global form of the object were consistent with a Gestalt-like "good form" (see Figure 4). We found evidence of unity perception in several such displays, suggesting that young infants can capitalize on multiple sources of information in these tasks, including, but not necessarily limited to, surface motion and configuration (see also Johnson, Bremner, Slater, Mason, & Foster, 2002).

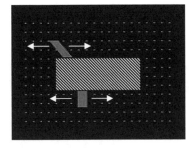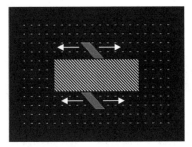

Figure 3. Stimuli used to test the role of edge alignment in 4-month-olds' perception of object unity. Adapted from Johnson and Aslin (1996).

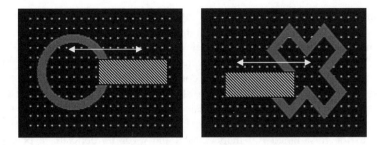

Figure 4. Stimuli used to test the role of "good form" in 4-month-olds' perception of object unity. Adapted from Johnson, Bremner, Slater, and Mason (2000).

1.4 Development of Perception of Trajectory Continuity

My colleagues and I have recently become interested in the question of how infants come to perceive events in which an object becomes fully occluded for a brief duration (Johnson, Bremner, Slater, Mason, Foster, & Cheshire, 2003). We adopted methods that were very similar to those employed to examine perception of object unity. Infants were first shown an event in which a ball moved back and forth cyclically, the center of its trajectory occluded by a box (see Figure 5, left). The infants then viewed test displays consisting either of the visible components only of the ball's trajectory seen during habituation (the *discontinuous* trajectory; Figure 5, right), or a *continuous* trajectory (which an adult would be likely to expect; Figure 5, center). We reasoned that if infants perceived the trajectory as continuous (and the ball as persistent under occlusion), then there would be a reliable preference for the discontinuous trajectory. On the other hand, a preference for the continuous trajectory test display would be taken as evidence that the infants perceived the habituation stimulus as consisting of disconnected motion paths. We found an intriguing pattern of results.

First, the likelihood of continuity perception in 4-month-olds was a function of occluder width (and, therefore, time the ball was out of sight).

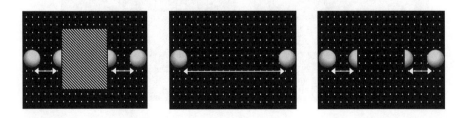

Figure 5. Stimuli used to test young infants' perception of the continuity of an object trajectory when its center portion was occluded. Adapted from Johnson, Bremner, Slater, Mason, Foster, and Cheshire (2003).

When 4-month-olds viewed displays with a narrow occluder, there was a reliable posthabituation preference for the discontinuous trajectory test display. In contrast, when 4-month-olds were habituated to a display with a relatively wide occluder, this preference reversed, implying perception of the visible path segments seen during habituation as unconnected.

Second, we tested both younger and older infants in this paradigm and found that 2-month-olds did not appear to perceive continuity even under the least demanding conditions we employed (i.e., the narrow occluder). In contrast, 6-month-olds provided evidence of continuity perception under the most challenging conditions (i.e., the wide occluder).

Consider the parallels in the outcomes of these experiments and studies of perception of object unity. We found age differences both in the ability to achieve perceptual completion in these tasks, and in the ability to overcome the challenges imposed by an occluder of varying widths. It is unknown, however, if the same mechanisms underlie success at the two kinds of task.

1.5 Mechanisms of Development

In the previous three sections of this chapter, I described experiments that have examined development of perception of object unity in infancy, experiments that have explored the kinds of visual cue used by infants to perceive unity, and experiments that have investigated infants' perception of the persistence of an object as it became fully occluded. The evidence reveals a general pattern across infancy from an initial processing of visual stimuli largely in terms of individual components, toward later processing of more global information, integrating the components across space and time (i.e., a shift from fragmented to holistic processing). How does this change occur? I consider three possibilities: changes in information-processing skills, as revealed by developments in eye movement strategies; the role of learning and experience; and neurophysiological development (see Johnson, 2001b for further details).

1.5.1 Eye Movements

The oculomotor system is sufficiently functional at birth such that neonates scan the environment systematically (Johnson, 2001a). Nevertheless, there are fundamental changes between 2 and 4 months in scanning "efficiently." Younger infants tend to fixate specific parts of the display, rather than all the visible surfaces (Johnson & Johnson, 2000). Figure 6 shows examples of younger (left) and older (right) infants' scan patterns when viewing rod-and-box displays. It remains unknown, however, how scanning patterns contribute to unity perception. It could be, for example, that infants learn about unity by frequent alternating fixations of the visible regions of partly occluded objects, a possibility that is currently under investigation.

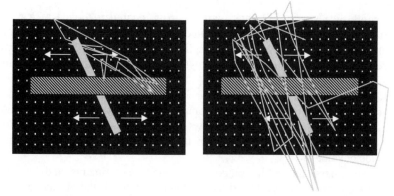

Figure 6. Examples of scanning patterns when infants viewed rod-and-box stimuli. The age difference is about 2 months. Notice how much more extensive are the scans produced by the older infant (at right). Adapted from Johnson and Johnson (2000).

1.5.2 Learning

Learning about occlusion might be a deductive process: multiple exposures to everyday events in which objects become occluded and then re-emerge, eventually leading to learning associations between views of objects as fully visible and partly occluded subsequent identification of partly occluded objects as continuous, via an associative process. Recently, Mareschal and I investigated the viability of this possibility with connectionist models that were presented with input representing moving objects and an occluder (Mareschal & Johnson, 2002). We then tested the models for their response to a partly occluded object as either unified or disjoint. The models were successful at responding to a partly occluded object as continuous, providing evidence for the possibility that a similar associative process might be at work in human infants in building object representations from multiple exposures of objects. This possibility remains to be tested in infants.

1.5.3 Neurophysiological Development

Perception of unity across a spatial gap may be accomplished with relatively low-level neural substrate (i.e., in cortical regions V1 and V2, the early visual areas), and development consists of at least two kinds of neural maturation. First, the long-range cell-to-cell interactions in these areas connect neural circuits that respond to similar edge orientations. These interactions may reach sufficient maturity within several months after birth to support unity perception under some circumstances. Second, there is a general reduction of neural "noise" (see Johnson, 2001b, in press). Perception of object persistence under occlusion may be centered more in higher visual areas that support neural activity coding for objects that have become occluded, such as inferotemporal cortex. One candidate mechanism that may underlie development of organized cortical activity in general is *neural synchrony*: Neural circuits that participate in a common goal engage in synchronized activity, firing in brief bursts in the 40 Hz range (Singer & Gray, 1995). There may be changes in synchronized activity in infants that are concomitants to perceptual development (Csibra, Davis, Spratling, & Johnson, 2000).

1.6 Development of Object Perception and Development of Face Perception

I have discussed evidence that development of object perception in infancy proceeds from an initial processing of fragments to a processing of wholes, that is, perceiving objects as continuous and complete across time and space. The question of fragmented vs. holistic perception is prominent also in research on face perception in infancy, and there is evidence for both kinds of processing, depending on the task.

1.6.1 Global-to-Local Preferences at Birth

Young infants' visual acuity is poor relative to that of adults, which means that discernment of fine details of visual stimuli is compromised (Atkinson, 2000). Poor acuity might be expected to induce a bias toward processing global features of a visual stimulus at the expense of local features, simply because global features are easier to see, and this is indeed the case. When global and local features are carefully placed in conflict, as when new features are presented either at the global or local level during a posthabituation test phase, newborn infants tend to respond principally to novel global stimuli, and pay less attention to novel local stimuli (Macchi Cassia, Simion, Milani, & Umiltà, 2002). This finding is consistent with the outcomes of experiments that examine newborn infants' preferences for the mother's face; such preferences appear to be abolished when information for outer facial contour and hair is masked with a scarf (Pascalis, de Schonen, Morton, Deruelle, & Fabre-Grenet, 1995). These findings might be taken as evidence that young infants have difficulty resolving the features of individual faces, but other evidence, reviewed in the next section, casts doubt on this hypothesis.

1.6.2 Face Discrimination at Birth

Despite neonates' poor acuity, there have been several convincing demonstrations that newborn infants distinguish different two-dimensional depictions of faces on the basis of internal features. For example, neonates prefer to look at attractive faces, implying discrimination of facial features that define (for adults) attractiveness (Slater, Bremner, Johnson, Sherwood, Hayes, & Brown, 2000). Evidence has emerged as well that neonates will discriminate different configurations of local elements if they are not pitted directly against global features, which tend to be strongly preferred (Macchi Cassia et al., 2002). Newborns discriminate schematic faces that consist of small elements (e.g., dark squares) arranged in either a facelike or non-facelike configuration, tending to prefer the facelike pattern (Simion, Farroni, Macchi Cassia, Turati, & Dalla Barba, 2002). These findings, along with results that document a global-to-local preference described in the previous section, suggest that young infants' processing of global vs. local stimulus elements is highly context dependent. The findings may be summarized as indicating that neonates can differentiate many kinds of detailed stimuli, but may fail to do so if there is competing, salient global stimulation, or if placed in an otherwise challenging circumstance.

1.6.3 What Determines Processing of Local or Global Features?

Simion and colleagues have presented an elegant series of reports that examined carefully the conditions under which newborn infants will prefer a facelike stimulus when paired with another stimulus with similar features, but arranged in a different configuration. They have found, for example, that neonates tend to prefer stimuli with more contours in their upper half, even if the preferred stimulus is not facelike (Turati, Simion, Milani, & Umiltà, 2002; Valenza, Simion, Macchi Cassia, & Umiltà, 1996). These preferences hold even when a facelike stimulus is pitted against a stimulus that is decidedly non-facelike, implying that face preferences may be rooted in a general up-down asymmetry in response. However, another study showed that orienting responses in newborns (i.e., looking toward the periphery) are stronger to facelike than other kinds of stimuli, suggesting that some sort of stored representation drives attention toward faces (Macchi Cassia, Simion, & Umiltà, 2001). In older infants (7-month-olds), processing of local elements vs. global configuration in faces has been found to depend on orientation of the stimulus. That is, there was an "inversion effect": Facial configuration was responded to more strongly when presented upright (Cohen & Cashon, 2001). Taken together, these findings and others indicate that early face perception is influenced by a combination of perceptual biases, both general (e.g., preferences for vertically asymmetrical stimuli) and specific (e.g., preferences for facelike configurations). Whether infants respond on the basis of local or global features depends on the nature of the task, but the important point for the present discussion is that both holistic and featural information guide face preferences from the onset of visual experience.

1.6.4 Face Versus Object Perception

The experiments reviewed in previous sections present contrasting evidence concerning young infants' processing of parts vs. wholes when viewing faces and objects. Face perception is guided from the start of postnatal life by both local and global information. This is true as well for object perception, but there is an important difference in the two perceptual tasks: The evidence to date indicates that very young infants (i.e., younger than 2 months) are not able to integrate visible surface fragments into holistic object percepts. In contrast, infants respond to facial configuration (i.e., holistic information) at birth. The difference between the two tasks is most likely due to the special nature of faces, which comprise a unique class of visual stimulus. Object perception is more challenging in some respects, due to the variegated nature of objects in the visual environment, and as a result, the developmental process of achieving general proficiency at perceiving occlusion is more protracted.

1.7 Conclusions

The progression from fragmented to holistic object perception is both radical and rapid. It is radical in that it may represent a complete shift in how infants perceive the world over the first several months after birth, from perceiving only what is directly visible toward an understanding of objects as continuous past the point of perceptual contact. This change is rapid in that it happens very quickly, relative to many other kinds of developmental change that occur in an individual's lifetime. We have a large descriptive database as a result of the dedicated efforts of many researchers over the past several years, but we lack firm evidence of precise mechanisms of these changes. These mechanisms are the focus of intense empirical efforts at present, and the outlook is very good for the emergence of fundamental new insights in the near term.

Acknowledgements

Support for preparation of this chapter was provided by NSF grant BCS-0094814 and NIH grant R01-HD40432.

References

Atkinson, J. (2000). *The developing visual brain*. Oxford, UK: Oxford University Press.
Bornstein, M. H. (1985). Habituation of attention as a measure of visual information processing in human infants: Summary, systematization, and synthesis. In G. Gottlieb & N. A. Krasnegor (Eds.), *Measurement of audition and vision in the first year of postnatal life: A methodological overview* (pp. 253-300). Norwood, NJ: Ablex.
Bower, T. G. R. (1967). Phenomenal identity and form perception in an infant. *Perception and Psychophysics, 2,* 74-76.
Cohen, L. B., & Cashon, C. H. (2001). Do 7-month-old infants process independent features or facial configurations? *Infant and Child Development, 10,* 83-92.
Csibra, G., Davis, G., Spratling, M. W., & Johnson, M. H. (2000). Gamma oscillations and object processing in the infant brain. *Science, 290,* 1582-1585.

Eizenman, D. R., & Bertenthal, B. I. (1998). Infants' perception of object unity in translating and rotating displays. *Developmental Psychology, 34*, 426-434.

Johnson, S. P. (2001a). Neurophysiological and psychophysical approaches to visual development. In A. F. Kalverboer & A. Gramsbergen (Series Eds.) & J. B. Hopkins (Section Ed.), *Handbook of brain and behaviour in human development: IV. Development of perception and cognition* (pp. 653-675). Amsterdam: Elsevier.

Johnson, S. P. (2001b). Visual development in human infants: Binding features, surfaces, and objects. *Visual Cognition, 8*, 565-578.

Johnson, S. P. (in press). Building knowledge from perception in infancy. To appear in L. Gershkoff-Stowe & D. Rakison (Eds.), *Building object categories in developmental time.* Mahwah, NJ: Hillsdale.

Johnson, S. P., & Aslin, R. N. (1995). Perception of object unity in 2-month-old infants. *Developmental Psychology, 31*, 739-745.

Johnson, S. P., & Aslin, R. N. (1996). Perception of object unity in young infants: The roles of motion, depth, and orientation. *Cognitive Development, 11*, 161-180.

Johnson, S. P., Bremner, J. G., Slater, A., & Mason, U. (2000). The role of good form in young infants' perception of partly occluded objects. *Journal of Experimental Child Psychology, 76*, 1-25.

Johnson, S. P., Bremner, J. G., Slater, A., Mason, U., & Foster, K. (2002). Young infants' perception of unity and form in occlusion displays. *Journal of Experimental Child Psychology, 81*, 358-374.

Johnson, S. P., Bremner, J. G., Slater, A., Mason, U., Foster, K., & Cheshire, A. (2003). Infants' perception of object trajectories. *Child Development, 74*, 94-108.

Johnson, S. P., Cohen, L. B., Marks, K. H., & Johnson, K. L. (in press). Young infants' perception of object unity in rotation displays. *Infancy.*

Johnson, S. P., & Johnson, K. L. (2000). Early perception-action coupling: Eye movements and the development of object perception. *Infant Behavior and Development, 23*, 461-483.

Johnson, S. P., & Náñez, J. E. (1995). Young infants' perception of object unity in two-dimensional displays. *Infant Behavior and Development, 18*, 133-143.

Jusczyk, P. W., Johnson, S. P., Spelke, E. S., & Kennedy, L. J. (1999). Synchronous change and perception of object unity: Evidence from adults and infants. *Cognition, 71*, 257-288.

Kellman, P. J. (1993). Kinematic foundations of infant visual perception. In C. E. Granrud (Ed.), *Visual perception and cognition in infancy* (pp. 121-173). Hillsdale, NJ: Erlbaum.

Kellman, P. J., & Spelke, E. S. (1983). Perception of partly occluded objects in infancy. *Cognitive Psychology, 15*, 483-524.

Kellman, P. J., Spelke, E. S., & Short, K. R. (1986). Infant perception of object unity from translatory motion in depth and vertical translation. *Child Development, 57*, 72-86.

Macchi Cassia, V., Simion, F., Milani, I., & Umiltà, C. (2002). Dominance of global visual properties at birth. *Journal of Experimental Psychology: General, 131*, 398-411.

Macchi Cassia, V., Simion, F., & Umiltà, C. (2001). Face preference at birth: The role of an orienting mechanism. *Developmental Science, 4*, 101-108.

Mareschal, D., & Johnson, S. P. (2002). Learning to perceive object unity: A connectionist account. *Developmental Science, 5*, 151-185.

Pascalis, O., de Schonen, S., Morton, J., Deruelle, C., & Fabre-Grenet, M. (1995). Mother's face recognition by neonates: A replication and an extension. *Infant Behavior and Development, 18*, 79-85.

Piaget, J. (1952). *The origins of intelligence in children.* New York: International Universities Press.

Simion, F., Farroni, T., Macchi Cassia, V., Turati, C., & Dalla Barba, B. (2002). Newborns' local processing in schematic facelike configurations. *British Journal of Developmental Psychology, 20*, 465-478.

Singer, W., & Gray, C. M. (1995). Visual feature integration and the temporal correlation hypothesis. *Annual Review of Neuroscience, 18,* 555-586.

Slater, A., Bremner, G., Johnson, S. P., Sherwood, P., Hayes, R., & Brown, E. (2000). Newborn infants' preference for attractive faces: The role of internal and external facial features. *Infancy, 1,* 265-274.

Slater, A., Johnson, S. P., Brown, E., & Badenoch, M. (1996). Newborn infants' perception of partly occluded objects. *Infant Behavior and Development, 19,* 145-148.

Slater, A., Morison, V., Somers, M., Mattock, A., Brown, E., & Taylor, D. (1990). Newborn and older infants' perception of partly occluded objects. *Infant Behavior and Development, 13,* 33-49.

Turati, C., Simion, F., Milani, I., & Umiltà, C. (2002). Newborns' preference for faces: What is crucial? *Developmental Psychology, 38,* 875-882.

Valenza, E., Simion, F., Macchi Cassia, V., & Umiltà, C. (1996). Face preference at birth. *Journal of Experimental Psychology: Human Perception and Performance, 22,* 892-903.

Address for Correspondence

Scott P. Johnson
Department of Psychology
Uris Hall
Cornell University
Ithaca, NY 14853
USA
E-mail: sj75@cornell.edu

Infants' Preference for Texture-Defined Targets of Different Saliency:
Evidence for Local Processing

Ruxandra Sireteanu

Irmgard Encke

Iris Bachert

2.1 Introduction

The human face is a prominent visual stimulus, known to attract the attention even of very young human infants. One of the most interesting questions is: What is this early attractiveness for the human face based upon? Do infants perceive the face as a whole – or do they process the individual features of the face separately, and bind them together at a later stage? One way to address these questions is to investigate the way infants process complex, two-dimensional, non-face stimuli. Our approach was to investigate the way infants segment visual stimuli in early life.

One aspect of visual segmentation is the segmentation of textures (Beck, 1966, 1982; Bergen & Julesz, 1983; Julesz, 1981, 1984). Textures consist of arrays of micropatterns containing a group of items that differ from the items of the background by a single feature. Sharp discontinuities between the different regions of the visual texture can often be perceived, while sometimes such discontinuities require careful scrutiny in order to be identified. The segmentation type depends on the kinds of elements within the region and on the relationship between these elements. If the group of discrepant elements can be detected immediately, its extraction is termed "preattentive." Elements supporting preattentive segmentation are known as "textons" (Bergen & Julesz, 1983; Julesz, 1981, 1984; for a modified list of textons, see Nothdurft, 1990, 1991, 1992). Preattentive texture segmentation was considered to proceed in parallel across the visual field, as opposed to a serial, element-by-element scrutiny by the searchlight of focal attention (but see Wolfe, 1992).

In the seventies, researchers started to ask how infants and children acquire these perceptual abilities. In 1975, Salapatek reviewed a series of experiments investigating the development of preferences for visual stimuli presented as matrices containing either a single discrepant element, or groups of discrepant elements. Monitoring the side of first fixation in a 30-second presentation period, he found that 2-month-old infants do not show the preference for discrepant objects characteristic of adult vision; this preference emerged somewhere between 2 months and 3 years of age. In some instances, 2-month-old infants even showed an intriguing *negative* preference, i.e., they oriented *away* from a discrepant stimulus (for example, a group of parallel line segments embedded in a matrix of squares). The infants tended to orient toward the side of the display containing *more squares*, regardless of whether the pattern elements were darker or brighter than the surround. Salapatek concluded that, during the earliest developmental stages, infants – unlike 3-year-old children – do not direct their gaze toward the discrepant target. The visual orienting behavior of the infants seemed to be governed by other factors, such as contour density, local brightness, or local shape.

Atkinson and Braddick (1992) presented infants with textures of obliquely oriented lines containing either a discrepant group of orthogonally oriented lines or a group with an increased density of lines, thus containing a luminance difference between target and background. The authors concluded that the segmentation of textures based on orientation differences emerges somewhere between 10 and 16 weeks of age and is slower to develop than segmentation based on luminance differences.

Sireteanu and Rieth (1992) investigated the development of texture segmentation in infants and children using textures containing either obliquely oriented line segments or dark blobs on a bright background. The target could be either a texture of an orthogonal orientation, or a group of blobs of a larger size than the surround. They found that segmentation of textures based on line orientation emerges at the end of the first year of life and does not become adult-like before school age; in contrast, segmentation of textures based on blob size was accomplished by infants as young as 2 months of age. Thus, although Sireteanu and Rieth agreed with Atkinson and Braddick that the segmentation of textures containing luminance differences occurs very early in life, and the segmentation of oriented textures requires a longer developmental period, they differed on the age of onset of the latter. This might be due to differences in the stimulus parameters, such as the size of the test field or of the discrepant patch (see Rieth & Sireteanu, 1994a, 1994b).

In the present study, we concentrate on another aspect governing visual preferences in adult observers, namely *visual saliency*. Schiller and Lee (1991) found that lesions in the extrastriate area V4 of the macaque monkey affect search for the "least salient" and the "most salient" item in a visual search task in different ways. The search for the most salient item seemed to be relatively unaffected, whereas the search for the least salient item was severely impaired. This result was independent of the stimulus feature (e.g., size, contrast, color saturation, or binocular disparity). This finding was recently corroborated by DeWeerd, Peralta III, Desimone, and Ungerleider (1999) who studied macaque monkeys with areas V4 and TEO lesioned.

The authors suggested that extrastriate areas like V4 and TEO might be involved in the processing of stimuli requiring selective attention.

To investigate the role of attention in visual search, Braun (1994) carried out an experiment in which adult human subjects attempted to carry out a letter discrimination task and a visual search task at the same time. He found that attentive adult observers were equally able to respond to both the most and the least salient object in the visual search task. If the attention of the subjects was engaged in a concurrent task, performance concerning the least salient item was severely impaired, while performance concerning the most salient item was only moderately affected. These results suggest that adults whose attention is engaged in a concurrent visual task might behave like monkeys lacking area V4. Taken together, Schiller's and Braun's results suggest that the search for the "least salient" and the "most salient" items represent fundamentally different types of visual tasks, with probably separate functional systems underlying their execution.

In this study, we wondered whether young infants might show different developmental time courses for the segmentation of targets which are more salient or less salient than their surround. To answer this question, we investigated the segmentation of textures with targets of different saliency. In Experiment I, we asked whether infants and children show comparable looking behavior toward the "most salient" and the "least salient" texture-defined target in a visual scene when tested in a forced-choice preferential looking situation. Sireteanu and Rieth (1992) had shown that infants were able to segment a texture consisting of larger blobs embedded in a background of smaller blobs, starting at least at 1 to 3 months of age. In this experiment, we wanted to know whether young infants also show a preference for the "least salient" target stimulus (defined by a smaller blob size than the surrounding elements). The stimuli of this experiment were presented on slides projected onto two separate test fields.

Three additional experiments were designed to make sure that the results of Experiment I were not due to the special configuration of the stimuli or to the procedure used in this experiment: In Control Experiment A, the forced-choice preferential looking procedure was replaced by a method of first fixation. In Experiment II, the texture stimuli were presented on a single, continuous test field, using cardboard cards. In Control Experiment B, the target textures were replaced by solid black or white squares presented on uniform gray cardboard cards.

All experiments were carried out using a preferential looking procedure. The underlying rationale of this method is that, if infants are able to detect a figure in an otherwise homogeneous background, this should lead to a preferential orienting of attention (and hence eye and head movements) towards the figure. We used a combination of the forced-choice preferential looking procedure (FPL: Dobson & Teller, 1978; Gwiazda, Brill, Mohindra, & Held, 1978; Teller, Morse, Borton & Regal, 1974) with stimuli presented on slides on two separate test fields (for details see also Sireteanu, 2000; Sireteanu, Encke, & Wagner, 2002; Sireteanu, Fronius, & Constantinescu, 1994; Sireteanu, Kellerer, & Boergen, 1984; Sireteanu & Rieth, 1992) and a preferential looking procedure with stimuli presented on cards, analogous to the Teller Acuity Card method (McDonald et al., 1996; see also Sireteanu, 2000; Sireteanu et al., 2002; Sireteanu and Rieth, 1992).

Only full-term infants and children with no developmental abnormalities were included in the data analysis. Prior to the experimental sessions, the subjects underwent a full orthoptic examination (visual acuity using the Teller Acuity Cards, cover test and eye motility for assessing the binocular status, Lang Test for measuring stereopsis, and refraction using the Cambridge VPR1 Paediatric Videorefractor). Subjects with visual disorders were referred to an ophthalmologist and excluded from the study. The subjects were recruited by announcements in family health care centers and at local pediatricians' offices. All subjects were naïve to the purpose and the procedure of the study. Informed consent was obtained from the parents after the procedure was explained fully.

2.2 Infants' Preference for Targets of Different Saliency (Experiment I)

In this experiment, we investigated whether infants and children known to have a preference for the "most salient" texture-defined target stimulus (a group of larger blobs in a background of smaller blobs) also orient reliably towards the "least salient" stimulus, a group of smaller blobs in a background of larger blobs.

For the "most salient" stimulus, the background stimulus was made of randomly arranged small black blobs of the same size (0.3° diameter, hitherto referred to as "small blobs") on a white background. The target stimulus contained a group of 4 × 4 neighboring blobs of a larger size (0.8° diameter, referred as "large blobs") standing out from the background of small blobs (see also Rieth & Sireteanu, 1994a, 1994b; Sireteanu & Rieth, 1992). The "least salient" stimulus consisted of a background stimulus made of large blobs. The target stimulus consisted of a group of 4 × 4 small blobs, embedded in a background of large blobs (see Figure 1).

SLIDE STIMULI

('most salient' vs. 'least salient' stimulus)

Figure 1. Stimuli used in Experiment I. Upper panel: "most salient" stimulus. Lower panel: "least salient" stimulus.

One stimulus side contained a figure embedded in a background; the other showed the background alone. Our parameters ensured that the stimuli were within the resolution limits of the youngest infants (Dobson & Teller, 1978; Sireteanu et al., 1984; Sireteanu, Fronius, & Constantinescu, 1994; Teller et al., 1974).

Testing took place in a darkened room. The chair for the parent or the subject (if old enough) was placed at a distance of 57 cm in front of a large wooden screen containing two circular apertures with a diameter of 15°, centered at 20° from the midline. The apertures were placed such that they approximated the infant's eye level. Mean luminance of the stimuli was 70 cd/m². Four red blinking lamps, two of which could be lit at a time, were arranged around a small central peephole (2° in diameter). The four small red blinking lamps served as a centering stimulus in between the trials. A video camera focusing on the infant's face was positioned behind the peephole.

Each session consisted of a minimum of 20 trials (for older children, 40 trials). On each trial, a pair of slides was projected from behind onto the two apertures. Four additional stimuli (drawings of faces, toys, animals), serving to maintain subjects' attention, were included in each 40-trial session. An adult observer, naïve to which configuration the child was seeing in each trial, looked at the subject's face on a video screen. The observer had to decide on the basis of the subject's looking behavior (side and duration of the first fixation, longest fixation, interested scanning, etc.) which side the subject preferred. The stimuli were presented in a pseudo-randomized order (not more than two identical stimuli in a row). At the end of the session, the percentage of correct responses was calculated. No preference corresponded to 50% correct. All sessions were judged in a "live" situation and also recorded on videotape. All sessions of this experiment were scored by the same observer (author I.E.).

We tested four groups of infants, each consisting of 12 subjects. Group I included infants between 1 and 3 months of age, Group II infants between 4 and 6 months, Group III infants between 7 and 9 months, and Group IV infants between 10 and 12 months. In addition, we examined 12 children aged 3 to 4 years. Each group contained roughly the equal number of girls and boys.

The percentage of correct responses of all infants to the "most salient" and the "least salient" stimulus is shown in Figure 2. All infants showed high, statistically significant ($p < 0.01$, one-sided Student t-test) preferences for the "most salient" stimulus. In contrast, none of these groups of infants showed a significant preference for the "least salient" stimulus. They looked at the side containing the "least salient" stimulus at chance level (52-55%).

In contrast, 3- to 4-year-old children preferred the side containing the "least salient" and the "most salient" stimulus highly significantly (74% and 78%, respectively; $p < 0.01$; Figure 3).

The finding that all infants showed statistically highly significant preferences for the "most salient" stimulus confirms the results of Sireteanu and Rieth (1992) and indicates that infants are able to detect the "most salient" stimulus in a visual scene as soon as 2 months of age. However, they do not show a preference for the "least salient" stimulus until somewhere between 1 year and approximately 3 or 4 years of age.

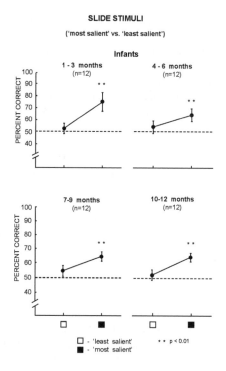

Figure 2. Results of Experiment I. Means and standard errors of percent correct responses for the "most salient" and the "least salient" stimulus in infants under 1 year of age.

2.2.1 The Role of the Experimental Procedure (Control Experiment A)

To make sure that the results of Experiment I, obtained with a forced-choice preferential looking procedure, can be replicated when using a first fixation procedure (as used by Salapatek in his 1975 study), the data from all 1- to 3-month-old infants and 3- to 4-year-old children included in Experiment I were reanalysed from the videotapes recorded during the experimental sessions, this time using a first fixation criterion. Previous experiments from our own laboratory had demonstrated that the forced-choice decision of a naïve observer did not differ between live and video-recorded material of the same experimental session, even when scored by different observers (Sireteanu, Neu, Fronius, & Constantinescu, 1998). The task of the observer was to decide from the videotaped material which side of the display subjects fixated first. A 30-second limitation was imposed on observation time. All scores were performed by the same observer (author I.E.) as in the forced-choice preferential looking condition in Experiment I. The scores were obtained from the 12 infants aged 1 to 3 months and the 12 children of 3 to 4 years of age included in the first experiment.

As expected, the "first fixation" method yielded results similar to those of the forced-choice preferential looking procedure (see broken lines in Figure 3). For the 1- to 3-month-old infants, preferences for the most salient stimulus were statistically highly significant (70%, $p < 0.01$) while for the least salient stimulus they were at chance level (57%, $p > 0.1$). For the 3- to 4-year-old children, both the "least salient" and the "most salient" stimulus yielded highly significant, positive responses (63% vs. 73%, statistically significant at the $p < 0.05$ and 0.01 level, respectively; Figure 3).

The percentage of correct responses of the 3- to 4-year-old children was definitely lower when using the first fixation procedure than with the forced-choice preferential looking method. This result is in line with the fact that the first fixation procedure yields preferences which are based on a peripheral location of the stimuli, while the forced-choice preferential procedure approximates a foveal positioning of the stimuli; a difference in the percentage of correct responses for either method was not expected in 1- to 3-month-old infants, since at this age the foveal specialization is still undeveloped (Hendrickson & Youdelis, 1984; see also Sireteanu, Fronius, & Constantinescu, 1994; Sireteanu, Kellerer, & Boergen, 1984). Thus, it seems that the finding of Experiment I is robust, and that the absence of preference for the least salient stimulus in 1- to 3-month-old infants is not due to the experimental procedure used.

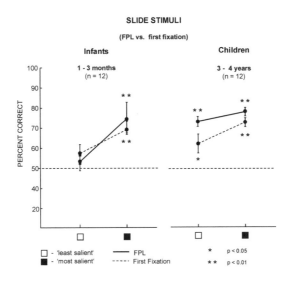

Figure 3. Results of Experiment I and Control Experiment A. *Continuous lines*: Percent correct responses for the "most salient" and the "least salient" stimulus in 1- to 3-month-old infants (data taken from Figure 2) and 3- to 4-year-old children, obtained with the forced-choice preferential looking procedure. *Broken lines*: Data from the same subjects, obtained with the method of first fixation.

2.3   The Role of the Experimental Set-Up (Experiment II)

To make sure that the results of Experiment I were not due to the presentation of the stimuli on two separate test fields rather than a single, continuous field, we performed an additional experiment, in which the stimuli were presented on a single test surface (Experiment II). The stimulus figure was embedded in a homogenous background of either small blobs ("most salient" stimulus) or large blobs ("least salient" stimulus). We used a modified preferential looking procedure. To enable a direct comparison with the results of Salapatek (1975), the observer had three alternatives: a) the child preferred the right side of the card; b) the child preferred the left side of the card; c) there was no preference. Thus, the response could be classified as a *hit* (the observer's guess was correct), a *miss* (the observer's guess was wrong) or a *tie* (no decision). In addition, the observers were asked to rate their confidence in the children's preferences. We reasoned that, if the results of Experiment I were independent of the configuration of the stimuli and the procedure used, they should be replicated in Experiment II.

The stimuli were presented on cardboard cards, 25 cm × 56 cm in size. This size, which replicates that of the Teller Acuity Cards (McDonald et al., 1996), was chosen in order to enable a direct comparison with the results of Sireteanu and Rieth (1992). For the same reason, the diameter of the small blobs was 0.6°, the diameter of the large blobs 1.6°. The "most salient" stimulus consisted of a group of 4 × 4 large blobs embedded in a background of small blobs. The "least salient" stimulus consisted of a group of 4 × 4 small blobs embedded in a background of large blobs (see Figure 4).

The subjects were tested in a well lit experimental room. The cards were presented in a gray three-sided wooden construction with a window the size of the cardboard cards. Mean luminance of the cards was 18 cd/m².

CARD STIMULI

('most salient' vs. 'least salient')

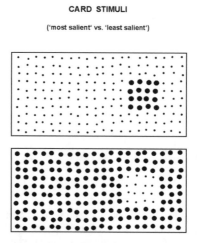

Figure 4. Stimuli used in Experiment II (card stimuli). Upper panel: "most salient" stimulus; lower panel: "least salient" stimulus.

We employed a modified preferential looking procedure. The child was held in front of the screen containing the opening in which the card was presented, hand-held by the observer at a distance of 57 cm. The observer, naïve to the side and the identity of the stimulus, looked at the child's face through a small peephole at the center of the card. Based on the subject's reaction and after having turned the card several times, she made a judgment on the subject's preferred side of the card. A second experimenter recorded in the protocol whether the target was on the preferred side or not. A correct answer from the observer was considered a "hit," a wrong answer a "miss," no answer a "tie." In addition, she rated her decision on a scale from 1 to 5, 1 meaning "very confident" and 5 meaning that she could not make a decision reliably. All observations were made by the same experimenter as in Experiment I and Control Experiment A (author I.E.). The subjects were 12 newly recruited infants of 1 to 3 months of age and 12 newly recruited children of 3 to 4 years of age.

The results of Experiment I were replicated in this experiment. All subjects preferred the side of the card containing the "most salient" stimulus. As in Experiment I, children of 3 to 4 years of age looked reliably at the "least salient" stimulus (11 out of 12 children, or 91,7%) whereas the group of young infants did not look at the "least salient" stimulus. Only two 1- to 3-month-olds (out of 12, or 16,7%) directed their attention toward the side of the card containing the least salient stimulus (see Figure 5).

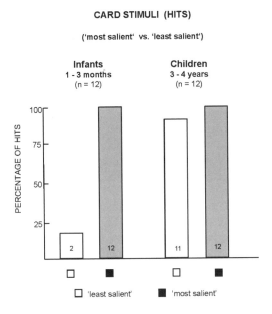

Figure 5. Results of Experiment II. Percentage of hits obtained in 1- to 3-month-old infants (left panel) and 3- to 4-year-old children (right panel) for texture-defined "most salient" (gray columns) and "least salient" stimuli (white columns). Figures indicate the actual number of subjects yielding hits.

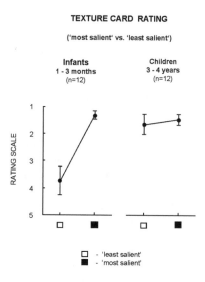

Figure 6. Confidence ratings for the "most salient" and the "least salient" stimulus in Experiment II. A rating score of 1 means "very confident," a rating score of 5 means "not confident." Each score is averaged over the subjects tested in each experimental group.

The results were confirmed by the confidence ratings given by the observer. For the 3- to 4-year-old children, confidence rates were close to 1 (very confident) for both the most salient and the least salient stimuli (1.50 for the most salient, 1.75 for the least salient). For the 1- to 3-month-old infants, the observer's ratings were very confident for the most salient stimulus (1.33), but were low for the least salient stimulus (3.75) (see Figure 6).

The results of this experiment indicate that the method of Experiment I yielded reliable results and that infants might not be able to detect the least salient stimulus.

Figures 5 and 6 refer to the percentages of correct responses ("hits") for both the "most salient" and the "least salient" stimulus. Figure 7 shows the responses of the children to the least salient stimulus, taking the three alternatives into account. At 1 to 3 months of age, infants generated the same number of hits and misses (16.7%), but the majority of their responses were ties (66.7%). Between 1 to 3 months and 3 to 4 years of age, the percentage of hits for the least salient stimulus increased dramatically, from 16.7% to 91.7%, while the percentage of ties decreased from 66.7% to 6.3% and the misses disappeared altogether.

Thus, the results of this experiment corroborate the results of Experiment I and Control Experiment A and show that the asymmetry in preference for the "most salient" and the "least salient" stimulus in young infants is not due to the configuration of the stimuli nor to the experimental procedure used. A further control experiment attempts to account for the role of luminance differences present in the above experiments.

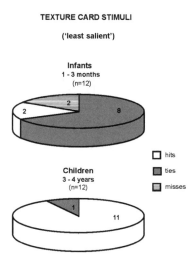

TEXTURE CARD STIMULI

('least salient')

Figure 7. Numbers of hits, misses and ties obtained with the "least salient" stimulus in 1- to 3-month-old infants (upper panel) and 3- to 4-year-old children (lower panel) in Experiment II.

2.3.1 *The Role of Luminance Differences (Control Experiment B)*

The stimuli in Experiments I and II and in Control Experiment A contained luminance differences. The "least salient" stimulus could have been perceived as a luminance decrement, i.e., a lighter square on a darker background whereas the "most salient" stimulus could have been seen as a darker square on a lighter background. This asymmetry might have caused a differential preference in the young infants.

To rule out that the results in these experiments were caused by these luminance differences, we tested infants and children with card stimuli representing luminance differences, but not containing texture-defined targets. To represent the "least salient" stimulus we showed a white square (10 cm × 10 cm) in a homogeneous gray background. For the "most salient" stimulus we showed a black square of the same size on a homogeneous gray background. The luminance of the gray background of the cards was halfway between the luminance of the solid black square and that of the white square (see Figure 8). We reasoned that, if infants and children responded to the luminance difference and not to the texture, they should prefer the solid black square but not the solid white square. If they showed a preference for both stimuli in this experiment, we could conclude that luminance differences do not account for the results of Experiments I and II.

We used the same apparatus and procedure as in Experiment II. All ratings were made by the same observer (author I.B.). The subjects were 12 newly recruited infants of 1 to 3 months of age.

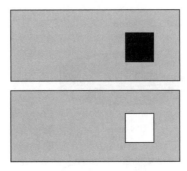

Figure 8. Stimuli used in Control Experiment B. Upper panel: solid black square. Lower panel: solid white square.

Eleven out of the 12 subjects (92%) preferred the black square, while 9 out of 12 (75%) showed a preference for the white square (right panel in Figure 9). There was no statistically significant difference in preference for the black over the white square. This result is in strong contrast to the pattern of preferences for the texture-defined "most salient" vs. "least salient" stimuli in Experiment II (for comparison purposes, the results of Experiment II are shown in the left panel in Figure 9).

Figure 10 shows the results of this control experiment, taking the three alternatives into account. Of the 12 infants tested in each condition, 9 yielded hits and 3 ties for the solid white square; there were 11 hits and 1 tie for the solid black square. There were no misses in this experiment. Again, there is a strong difference between these results and those of Experiment II (compare Figure 10 with Figure 7).

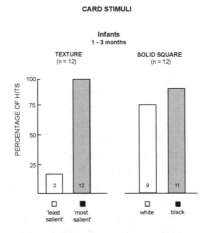

Figure 9. Results of Control Experiment B. Right panel: Number of hits obtained by 1- to 3-month-old infants for a solid black square (gray columns) or a solid white square (white columns). For comparison, the results of Experiment II with texture-defined stimuli are shown in the left panel.

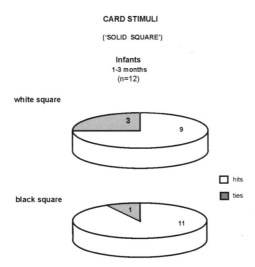

Figure 10. Numbers of hits, misses and ties obtained in 1- to 3-month-old infants with the stimuli from Control Experiment B. No misses were recorded in this experiment. Upper panel: solid white square; lower panel: solid black square.

Taken together, the results of Experiments I and II can be explained by processes of texture segmentation and not by differences in luminance between target and background.

2.4 General Discussion

The lack of preference of the infants for the "least salient" stimulus confirmed that infants, to a certain extent, behave like Braun's non-attentive or distracted adults (both are reminiscent of Schiller & Lee's macaque monkeys lacking Area V4).

The results of our experiments corroborate Salapatek's (1975) finding that young infants do not show a preference for the "least salient" texture-defined visual object. However, we did not replicate his suggestion that infants might have a *negative* preference for the "least salient" stimulus (in his case, a group of parallel line segments embedded in a matrix of squares) and that this preference might be replaced by an adult-like, positive preference for the discrepant texture by the third year of life. While our 3- to 4-year-olds showed a positive preference both for the "most salient" and the "least salient" stimulus, we found that 1- to 3-month-old infants disregarded our "least salient" stimulus.

This cannot be attributed to the different procedures used in the two studies, since we replicated our results with the method of first fixation, used in Salapatek's study. It is possible that our stimuli and those used by Salapatek were not entirely equivalent: The elements in his target stimulus differed from those of the surround not only in brightness but also in the amount and complexity of the contour. In our case, the items of the target (small blobs) differed from those of the background (large blobs) mainly in local brightness. Thus, one of the reasons suggested by Salapatek – namely contour density – might have been responsible for the reverse preference seen in his study.

Another explanation might involve the different attentional requirements of the stimuli: In our study, the infants' attention might have been attracted by both the individual large blobs (local luminance cue) as well as the texture border between the large and the small blobs (contour cue). With the "most salient" stimulus, both cues are located on the same side of the display and thus command a clear preference for this side. With the "least salient" stimulus, the two attentional attractors are located on opposite sides of the experimental array, and thus create a conflicting situation. With increasing age, the attentional weight of the contour border might increase, and thus enable an overt orienting reaction toward the side with the discrepant patch. (This tentative explanation might also accommodate Salapatek's results: It could be that the relative dominance of the background squares over the single lines used in his experiments might exceed that of the larger over the smaller blobs used in our experiments, thus giving rise to a negative preference.) This possibility supports the finding of our previous experiments (Rieth & Sireteanu, 1994a, 1994b; Sireteanu & Rieth, 1992) that in young infants, local attentional cues dominate over global ones, thus pointing to a late development of coherence and binding in the human visual system.

Preference for global shape emerges somewhere between 1 and 3 years of age, indicating the emergence of neural mechanisms involved in the "binding" of visual features to form coherent figures. These mechanisms are known to involve visual attention. A good candidate for the neural substrate of these mechanisms might be the long-range, tangential fibers in the primary visual cortex, which are known to emerge after birth and take several years to reach maturity (Burkhalter, Bernardo, & Charles, 1993; suggestion put forward by Sireteanu & Rieth, 1992; see also Atkinson & Braddick, 1992; Kovacs, 2000; Sireteanu, 2000, 2001).

Experimental support for this assumption comes from an independent line of research in our laboratory which shows that infants' performance in a visual search paradigm is qualitatively different from that of adult observers. Again, the adult pattern of visual preferences becomes manifest somewhere between the first and the third year of life (Sireteanu & Wagner, 2002; Sireteanu, Wagner, & Bachert, 2001).

The suggestion that infants seem to be more attracted by salient stimuli on a local scale than by the global shape of a group of stimuli receives independent support from a recent study on infants' perception of faces, which indicates that infants might be excellent "analysts," but poor "synthesizers": Indeed, infants are able to identify single facial features before they are able to identify faces as a whole (Schwarzer, 2000; see also Chapter 4).

Acknowledgements

We would like to thank all parents of the infants and children who participated in this study. This research was supported by grants from the Deutsche Forschungsgemeinschaft (Si 344/11-1, 2). We wish to express our gratitude to Professor Wolf Singer for his hospitality, encouragement, and support. Thanks are due to Dr. Regina Rettenbach for significant contributions in the early stages of the study and to Manuela Wagner for her contribution in the later stages of the work.

References

Atkinson, J., & Braddick, O. (1992). Visual segmentation of oriented textures by infants. *Behavioural Brain Research, 49,* 123-131.

Beck, J. (1966). Effect of orientation and shape similarity in perceptual grouping. *Perception & Psychophysics, 1,* 300-392.

Beck, J. (1982). Textural segmentation. In J. Beck (Ed.), *Organization and Representation in Perception* (pp. 285-317). Hillsdale, NJ: Erlbaum.

Bergen, J. R., & Julesz, B. (1983). Parallel versus serial processing in rapid pattern discrimination. *Nature, 303,* 696-698.

Braun, J. (1994). Visual search among items of different salience: Removal of attention mimics a lesion in extrastriate area V4. *Journal of Neuroscience, 14 (2),* 554-567.

Burkhalter, A., Bernardo, K. L., & Charles, V. (1993). Development of local circuits in human visual cortex. *Journal of Neuroscience, 13,* 1916-1931.

DeWeerd, P., Peralta III, M. R., Desimone, R., & Ungerleider, L. G. (1999). Loss of attentional stimulus selection after extrastriate cortical lesions in macaques. *Nature Neuroscience, 2 (8),* 753-758.

Dobson, V., & Teller, D. Y. (1978). Visual acuity in human infants: A review and comparison of behavioural and electrophysiological studies. *Vision Research, 18,* 1469-1483.

Gwiazda, J., Brill, S., Mohindra, I., & Held, R. (1978). Infant visual acuity and its meridional variation. *Vision Research, 18,* 1557-1564.

Hendrickson, A., & Youdelis, C. (1984). The morphological development of the human fovea. *Ophthalmology, 91,* 603-612.

Julesz, B. (1981). Textons, the elements of texture perception, and their interactions. *Nature, 290,* 91-97.

Julesz, B. (1984). A brief outline of texton theory of human vision. *Trends in Neuroscience, 7,* 41-45.

Kovacs, I. (2000). Human development of perceptual organization. *Vision Research, 40,* 1301-1311.

McDonald, M., Dobson, V., Sebris, S. L., Baitch, L., Varner, D., & Teller, D. Y. (1996). The acuity card procedure: A rapid test of infant acuity. *Investigative Ophthalmology & Visual Science, 26,* 1158-1162.

Nothdurft, C. (1990). Texton segregation by associated differences in global and local luminance distribution. *Proceedings of the Royal Society London, B 239,* 295-320.

Nothdurft, C. (1991). Texture segmentation and pop-out from orientation contrast. *Vision Research, 31,* 1073-1078.

Nothdurft, C. (1992). Feature analysis and the role of similarity in preattentive vision. *Perception and Psychophysics, 52 (4),* 355-375.

Rieth, C., & Sireteanu, R. (1994a). Texture segmentation and "pop-out" in infants and children: The effect of test field size. *Spatial Vision, 8,* 173-191.

Rieth, C., & Sireteanu, R. (1994b). Texture segmentation and visual search based on orientation contrast: An infant study with the familiarization-novelty preference method. *Infant Behaviour and Development, 17,* 359-369.

Salapatek, P. (1975). Pattern perception in early infancy. In L. Cohen & P. Salapatek (Eds.), *Handbook of Infant Perception: From Sensation to Cognition,* Vol. I. New York: Academic Press.

Schiller, P., & Lee, K. (1991). The role of primate extrastriate area V4 in vision. *Science, 251,* 1251-1253.

Schwarzer, G. (2000). Development of face processing: The effect of face inversion. *Child Development, 71,* 391-401.

Sireteanu, R. (2000). Texture segmentation, "pop-out" and feature binding in infants and children. In C. Rovee-Collier, L. Lipsitt, & Hayne, H. (Eds.), *Advances in Infancy Research, Vol. I* (pp. 183-249). Mahwah, New Jersey: Erlbaum Academic Publisher.

Sireteanu, R. (2001). Development of the visual system in the human infant. In A. F. Kalverboer & A. Gramsbergen (Eds.), *Handbook of Brain and Behaviour in Human Development* (pp. 629-652). London: Kluwer Academic Publishers.

Sireteanu, R., Encke, I., & Wagner, M. (2002). Saliency and context play a role in infants' texture segmentation. Manuscript in preparation.

Sireteanu, R. Fronius, M., & Constantinescu, D. H. (1994). The development of visual acuity in the peripheral visual field of human infants: Binocular and monocular measurements. *Vision Research, 34,* 1659-1671.

Sireteanu, R., Kellerer, R., & Boergen, K.-P. (1984). The development of peripheral visual acuity in human infants: A preliminary study. *Human Neurobiology, 3,* 81-85.

Sireteanu, R., Neu, B., Fronius, M., & Constantinescu, D. H. (1998). Live vs. video observation in forced-choice preferential looking: A comparison of methods. *Strabismus, 6 (2),* 81-86.

Sireteanu, R., & Rieth, C. (1992). Texture segregation in infants and children. *Behavioural Brain Research, 49,* 133-139.

Sireteanu, R., & Wagner, M. (2002). Looking for visual primitives: Visual search in infants and children. Manuscript in preparation.

Sireteanu, R., Wagner, M., & Bachert, I. (2001). What features do little creatures look at? *Investigative Ophthalmology & Visual Science, 42 (4),* p. 122.

Teller, D. Y., Morse, R., Borton, R., & Regal, D. (1974). Visual acuity for vertical and diagonal gratings in human infants. *Vision Research, 14,* 1433-1439.

Wolfe, J. (1992). "Effortless" texture segmentation and "parallel" visual search are not the same thing. *Vision Research, 32,* 757-763.

Address for Correspondence

Ruxandra Sireteanu
Department of Biological Psychology   *and*   Department of Neurophysiology
Institute for Psychology   Max Planck Institute for Brain Research
Johann Wolfgang Goethe-University Frankfurt   Deutschordenstr. 46
Mertonstr. 17   D-60528 Frankfurt/M.
D-60054 Frankfurt/M.   Germany
Germany   E-mail:sireteanu@mpih-frankfurt.mpg.de

3

Development of Depth and Object Perception in Infancy

Michael Kavšek

3.1 Introduction

This chapter deals with research on infants' ability to react to depth cues and to employ these cues to extract the spatial characteristics of the objects in the visual world. James Gibson's ecological approach to visual perception (e.g., Gibson, 1979) had a lasting effect on this research area by emphasizing the meaning of the structural components of our visual surroundings for perception. More specifically, Gibson maintains that visual information is directly "picked up" rather than "processed." Instead of investigating how the visual system functions, that is, how it works out space and object perception, he systematically describes the many different constituents that are part of the light reaching the eyes and that provide us with information on the spatial structure of the physical world. In particular, Gibson delineates both the depth information produced by movement of the observer and by motion of objects and the spatial information embedded in the static structure of the visual world.

All in all, current research assumes that distance and three-dimensional form can be extracted from kinetic information (e.g., Ullman, 1979), from pictorial depth cues (e.g., Hochberg, 1971), from oculomotor cues, specifically convergence and accommodation (e.g., Gillam, 1995), and from binocular disparity (e.g., Arditi, 1986). In the past few decades, developmental researchers have taken up the question of when during the first year of life infants begin to respond to the spatial meaning of the different depth cues. Studies on the ability to extract a depth stratification of surfaces from kinematic, binocular, oculomotor and pictorial depth signals are listed in Table 1. An overview of studies on object perception using depth cues is available in Table 2.

3.2 Kinematic Depth and Object Perception

According to many theories, spatiotemporal variation in the visual array is fundamental to human vision (e.g., Johansson, 1970). Kinematic depth information is based upon movement of the observer as well as of objects. It can be shown that motion is very effective in revealing the depth stratification of surfaces and the three-dimensional structure of objects (e.g., Braunstein, 1976).

Many studies substantiate that infants are able to exploit kinematic information in order to ascertain a variety of properties of our surroundings. For example, several investigations conclude that 4- and even 2-month-olds perceive the connectedness of the visible portions of a partially occluded object if these portions share a common motion (e.g., Eizenman & Berthenthal, 1998; Johnson & Aslin, 1995; Kellman & Spelke, 1983). Other studies suggest that the ability to perceive the structure of the human body revealed through biomechanical motion is present early in infancy (e.g., Bertenthal, 1993) and that specific optic flow patterns elicit postural compensations in newborn babies (e.g., Jouen & Lepecq, 1989). Furthermore, 3-month-old infants can infer the elasticity versus rigidity of an object from deforming versus rigid patterns of motion (e.g., Walker, Owsley, Megaw-Nyce, Gibson, & Bahrick, 1980).

3.2.1 Kinematic Depth Perception

The extraction of depth from motion occurs very early in development. From about 1 month of age onwards, babies react to *looming* information, that is, to the symmetrical expansion of the contour of an approaching object specifying impending collision (e.g., Ball & Vurpillot, 1976; Náñez & Yonas, 1994).

If an object approaches, this change is accompanied not only by a symmetrical expansion of the object's contour, but also by a magnification of the texture elements on its own surface and by the covering up of texture elements of the background. Gibson (1982) reports on a study on the ability of 3-month-old infants to differentiate between an approaching object and an approaching aperture. Though also containing an expanding contour, an approaching aperture is accompanied by *accretion of background texture* inside its contour. The information provided by an approaching aperture signals a safe situation, that is, an opening through which one can pass, whereas the information produced by an approaching obstacle specifies a danger to be avoided. According to the results, measures of head pressure indicated that the babies pulled back their heads as the solid object approached but did not so as the aperture approached. Schmuckler and Li (1998) established that disocclusion of background texture was the basis of 3-month-olds' ability to distinguish between approaching obstacles and approaching apertures. In their experiment, they manipu-lated the salience of the background. Instead of observing head pressure, they used eye blinks as a measure for the infant's ability to detect impending collision. If the infants' reaction to impending collision with a solid object depends mainly on symmetrical expansion of the object's contour and on texture expansion within the obstacle's contour, varying the salience of the background should not influence infants' eye blinks. However, the salience of the background should influence reactions to an approaching aperture. Increasing the background's salience strengthens the information provided by accretion of background texture within the aperture's contour, that is, the possibility of passage. In consequence, the dangerous situation signaled by the symmetrical expansion of the aperture's contour and by texture expansion within the aperture's frame will be increasingly diminished. This should result in a reduction of the defensive eye blink reaction. All predictions were confirmed by the findings of the study: The participants responded more to approaching obstacles than to apertures. Moreover, the reaction to looming apertures, but not to looming solid objects, was inversely related to the salience of the back-ground surface. The results confirm the role of symmetrical expansion of an object and of the enlargement of texture on the object as crucial factors that can be exploited by 3-month-old infants to discern the approach of a body. Furthermore, the findings provide evidence that young infants differentiate approaching apertures from approaching obstacles on the basis of the presence or absence of accretion of back-ground texture inside the object's contour.

Not only does covering up or uncovering of texture elements of the background indicate changes in distance of an object from the observer, but it can also reveal lateral motion of a surface across a background. More specifically, if a front surface moves across a background surface, its leading edge will progressively wipe out texture elements on the background surface, while its trailing edge will progressively reveal texture elements on the surface behind it. Research conducted by Granrud, Yonas, Smith, Arterberry, Glicksman, and Sorknes (1984) has tested young infants' ability to detect the relative depth ordering of two surfaces from accretion and deletion of texture. In this study, infants of 5 and 7 months of age were presented with computer-generated random-dot displays in which accretion and deletion of texture provided information about a foreground surface moving in front of a back-ground surface. Both the 5- and the 7-month-old participants reached more often for the apparently nearer area on the display than for the surface specified as farther. Since by 4 to 5 months of age infants begin to reach more frequently for the nearer of two surfaces if they perceive a depth difference (Yonas & Granrud, 1985a; Yonas & Hartman, 1993), Granrud et al. concluded that 5-month-old infants are sensitive to accretion and deletion of texture and use this as 3D information about the spatial layout of surfaces.

Later, Craton and Yonas (1988) pointed out that the display used by Granrud et al. (1984) not only contained accretion and deletion of texture, but also an additional kinetic depth cue, *boundary flow*. When one surface moves across a background surface, the texture of the foreground surface moves with the edge of this surface. In contrast, the texture elements of the background texture move in a direction different from that of the foreground edge. In their study, Craton and Yonas presented 5-

month-old infants two-dimensional displays in which the texture elements on both the foreground and the background surface were separated by a blank space. This blank space made it possible to eliminate accretion and deletion of texture from the experimental display, leaving boundary flow as the only cue specifying two surfaces at different depths. Participants displayed a significant reaching preference for the surface which appeared to be nearer. This result shows that 5-month-olds use boundary flow information at edges as a depth cue.

Table 1. Overview of studies on sensitivity to kinematic, oculomotor, binocular, and pictorial depth signals.

	Studies	*Age at which sensitivity to the depth signal has been demonstrated*
Perception of depth from kinematic information		
• looming information	e.g., Ball & Vurpillot (1976), Náñez & Yonas (1994)	1 month of age
• symmetrical expansion of an object + enlargement of texture on the object	Gibson (1982), Schmuckler & Li (1998)	3 months of age
• boundary flow + accretion and deletion of texture	Granrud, Yonas, Smith, Arterberrry, Glicksman, & Sorknes (1984)	5 months of age
• boundary flow	Craton & Yonas (1988)	5 months of age
• motion parallax	von Hofsten, Kellman, & Putaansuu (1992)	3½ months of age
• concurrent motion	Kellman, von Hofsten, & Soares (1987)	3½ months of age
Perception of depth from binocular disparity	e.g., Granrud (1986)	4 months of age
Perception of depth from convergence	von Hofsten (1977)	4 to 7 months of age
Perception of depth from accommodation	–	–
Perception of depth from pictorial depth cues		
• linear perspective, texture gradients, relative size, familiar size, shading, surface contour information, interposition	e.g., Granrud & Yonas (1984), Yonas, Granrud, Arterberry, & Hanson (1986)	7 months of age
• line junctions	Kavšek (1999), Yonas & Arterberry (1994)	8 months of age
	e.g., Bhatt & Bertin (2001)	3 months of age

According to Craton and Yonas (1988), infants are able to perceive the order of depth of surfaces from boundary flow by 5 months of age. This result casts doubt on the observation made by Granrud et al. (1984) that 5-month-olds react to accretion and deletion of texture. It is possible that this result is based on infants' sensitivity to boundary flow information instead. However, Schmuckler and Li (1998) provided evidence for young infants' ability to respond to accretion of background texture as a cue to depth. Other research leads one to suppose that 3½-month-olds are sensitive to *motion parallax* (von Hofsten, Kellman, & Putaansuu, 1992) as well as to *concurrent motion* (Kellman, von Hofsten, & Soares, 1987) as depth signals.

3.2.2 Kinematic Object Perception

Accretion and deletion of texture can also be used by young infants to perceive object form in two-dimensional displays. Kaufmann-Hayoz, Kaufmann, and Stucki (1986) confronted 3-month-old infants with random-dot displays. Each display consisted of a random-dot background onto which a surface was placed that was also covered with random-dot texture. If stationary, the surface was camouflaged. When in motion, however, the form of the surface became visible. The kinetic information responsible for 2D shape to appear is accretion and deletion of texture. Kaufmann-Hayoz et al. found that their participants were capable of discriminating between different kinetic shapes (see also Spitz, Stiles, & Siegel, 1993). Johnson and Mason (2002) extended these findings to 2-month-old infants. Interestingly, they emphasize that the infants' performance can be traced back to either extraction of accretion and deletion of texture, extraction of boundary flow, or perception of both factors. By systematically varying the kinetic information specifying illusory form, Johnson and Mason could provide evidence that their participants could perceive surface shape from both accretion and deletion of texture in conjunction with luminance information and boundary flow.

Motion-carried information is also a highly effective source of information for the characteristics of 3D objects. Research conducted by Kellman and his colleagues indicates that at about 4 months of age infants can perceive three-dimensional shape from transforming optical projections, but not from single or multiple static views of an object. Kellman (1984) habituated 4-month-old infants to a videotaped display of a single three-dimensional object rotating around two different axes on alternate trials. During the posthabituation trials, infants saw the same object moving around a new axis of rotation in depth and a new three-dimensional object, also rotating around the same new axis. Infants generalized habituation to the familiar object, but not to the novel shape. Furthermore, they dishabituated significantly to the novel object. The solid bodies in this study, however, were illuminated primarily from one direction. Kellman (1993) discusses that object discrimination in the study might be provoked by changes in brightness and texture gradients, instead of being caused by transformations of perspective of object edges. Therefore, Kellman and Short (1987, Exp. 3A) used rotating wire outlines of forms. Since these wire objects have no surfaces, transformations of surface brightness and texture are absent. Indeed, results showed that apart from surface information, continuous transformations of perspective of an object's bounding contours could indicate 3D structure to 4-month-old infants.

Besides providing kinetic information for three-dimensional object form, rotating the experimental shapes serves yet another purpose. Presenting just a single stationary view of a 3D object implies that only one particular 2D projection is transferred to the infant's eye. If, therefore, after habituation to a single view of a 3D shape, the participants dishabituate to a novel 3D object, one cannot conclude unequivocally that this behavior is based on 3D form discrimination. It is equally possible that the infants' visual response is a result of the differences between the 2D projections of the novel object and the original object. According to Kellman (1993), altering the two-dimensional retinal images of the experimental displays by presenting them in different spatial orientations, that is, by rotating them around various axes, prevents the infants from concentrating on particular 2D projections as the basis of response. Instead, they are compelled to pay attention to 3D form. However, Shaw, Roder, and Bushnell (1986) criticize that it is nevertheless possible that infants react on the basis of 2D information rather than on the basis of 3D form from transformations of linear perspective. For example, the rotating wire outlines in the Kellman and Short (1987, Exp. 3A) experiment might have been distinguished by detecting the different angle sizes between the lines which formed the experimental objects. At first glance, this argumentation seems to be convincing. However, Shaw et al. disregard the fact that the wire figures used by Kellman and Short were designed so that the proximal differences between them were minimal. Secondly, both 4-month-old and adult control groups (Kellman & Short, 1987, Exps. 3A and 3B) could not discriminate between the experimental objects when confronted with multiple static views taken from the rotation sequences. If indeed the infants' discrimination of the continuously rotating 3D structures arose from similarities of the 2D properties of the experimental stimuli, this discriminatory performance should have been generalized to multiple static views of the stimuli as well. Thirdly, the axis of rotation was changed from the habituation period to the posthabituation trials, thereby ensuring that the proximal views and transforming patterns in the dishabituation phase were different from the 2D views and motion patterns in the habituation period.

In the light of these arguments, it is plausible to assume that the experimental evidence indicates that the ability of 4-month-old infants to distinguish between 3D structures is driven by continuous optical transformations of these structures. Unfortunately, one might still object that while it is true that 4-month-old infants are not capable of discerning 2D differences between stimuli from multiple static views, the infants' discriminatory performance is improved if the proximal differences are embedded in motion displays. That is, it is possible that the infants respond to kinetic figural aspects of the stimuli, rather than to 3D object shape. Therefore, Arterberry and Yonas (1988) employed kinetic computer-generated random-dot displays that, when stationary, appeared as a random array of dots without any shape. When in motion, however, the displays appeared as either an incomplete or a complete cube. Hence, the only information specifying differences in 3D object structure in these stimuli was the motion of the randomly arranged dots. Arterberry and Yonas found that 4-month-old infants could discriminate the experimental stimuli. But again, although strongly suggesting that the infants perceived the 3D structure from optic flow information, the result does not rule out the possibility that the infants detected the various velocities within the displays, rather than the distal shapes specified by motion-carried information. In a further study, Arterberry and Yonas (2000) succeeded in showing that even 2-month-old infants are sensitive to optic flow information specifying 3D object shape. Moreover, the objection that the infants attended solely to the differential velocities of the dots making up the stimuli was disproved by an appropriate control condition (see also Arterberry, 1992).

Table 2. Overview of studies on extraction of object structure from kinematic, oculomotor, binocular, and pictorial depth cues.

	Studies	*Age at which object perception from the depth signal has been demonstrated*
Object perception from kinematic information	Schmuckler & Proffitt (1994)	5 months of age
	Arterberry (1992), Arterberry & Yonas (1988), Kellman (1984, 1993), Kellman & Short (1987, Exp. 3A)	4 months of age
	Arterberry & Yonas (2000)	2 months of age
	Kaufmann-Hayoz, Kaufmann, & Stucki (1986)	3 months of age: perception of 2D shape from boundary flow + accretion and deletion of texture
	Johnson & Mason (2002)	2 months of age: perception of 2D shape from either boundary flow, accretion and deletion of texture or both factors
Perception of depth from binocular information	Shaw, Roder, & Bushnell (1986)	6 months of age ("transfer-across-depth-cues"-paradigm)
	Owsley (1983, Exp. 1), Yonas, Arterberry, & Granrud (1987a)	4 months of age ("transfer-across-depth-cues"-paradigm)
	Ruff (1978)	9 months of age
Object perception from convergence	–	–
Object perception from accommodation	–	–
Object perception from pictorial depth cues	Kavšek (2001)	9 months of age

Taken together, these studies provide converging evidence that the extraction of depth and 3D object shape occurs very early in development. On the other hand, it also becomes clear that this claim is difficult to justify: Although Arterberry and Yonas (2000) excluded the possibility that the 2-month-old participants in their investigation reacted on the basis of velocity differences, it can not be ruled out that the infants detected the various patterns of motion characteristics within the different stimuli. It should be noted at this point that all research on infant 3D object perception is inevitably faced with the problem that 3D and 2D perception might be compounded (see also Schmuckler & Proffitt, 1994). Since 2D properties cannot be eliminated from a 3D object, it cannot be ruled out that object discrimination originates from the extraction not only of 3D cues but also of proximal structure. The studies described in this section, however, demonstrate that one can minimize the 2D information available in the experimental stimuli. For example, one measure to prevent the infants from discriminating the experimental displays by means of certain proximal cues is to oscillate the stimuli about different axes. Similarly, in research on the extraction of 3D object structure from binocular and pictorial depth information, one can present the experimental displays in different static spatial orientations. By altering the two-dimensional retinal image of the stimuli, one can prevent the infants reacting to the differences between the single 2D projections of the habituation and the novel object.

3.3 Binocular Depth and Object Perception

Stereopsis is a very accurate visual source of information about three-dimensionality. Stereoscopic information stems from a comparison of the images obtained from the two eyes. Each eye sees a slightly different view of the world due to the horizontal separation of the eyes. This *binocular disparity* can be used as a highly effective cue to depth: Objects at different distances project to disparate locations in the two eyes.

3.3.1 *Binocular Depth Perception*

There is general agreement that sensitivity to binocular disparity emerges suddenly somewhere between 3 and 5 months of age (e.g., see Birch, 1993). Furthermore, the emergence of this ability is obviously accompanied by the onset of stereoscopic depth perception (e.g., Fox, Aslin, Shea, & Dumais, 1980; Gordon & Yonas, 1976; Granrud, 1986). For example, Granrud (1986) found that by 4 months of age disparity-sensitive infants display a significantly more accurate spatial perception than do binocular-insensitive infants.

3.3.2 Binocular Object Perception

Evidence for infants' use of stereoscopic depth information for the detection of 3D object structure has been achieved within the "transfer-across-depth-cues" paradigm (Yonas & Pick, 1975). According to the design of this paradigm, infants are typically habituated to a rotating object, the 3D structure of which is provided by transformations of linear perspective, and are tested afterwards with stationary objects, the spatial shape of which is specified by binocular information. The purpose of this procedure is again to distract the infants' attention from proximal stimulus properties by changing these properties from the habituation to the dishabituation trials. Both Owsley (1983, Exp. 1) and Yonas, Arterberry, and Granrud (1987a) found evidence for 4-month-olds' ability to transfer object shape from kinetic to binocular information. In contrast, Shaw et al. (1986) reported that 6-month-olds, but not younger infants, succeeded in solving this transfer task.

If, however, all the information from optical transformations is removed from both the habituation and the dishabituation period, younger infants fail to show significant dishabituation behavior (Cook, Birch, & Griffiths, 1986; Kellman, 1993; Kellman & Short, 1987, Exp. 2; Ruff, 1978). Kellman and Short (1987, Exp. 2) habituated both 4- and 6-month-old participants to multiple stationary views of a real 3D object and then tested them with stationary views of the same object and of a novel object, both of which rotated around a different axis to those employed in the habituation trials. Despite the availability of both pictorial and binocular 3D information, both age groups showed no reliable dishabituation pattern. Kellman (1993) reports that this result can be extended to infants of 7½ months of age. Most importantly, Ruff (1978) established that 6-month-old infants failed to recognize a shape in a new orientation if they had previously been familiarized with the object in various stationary orientations. Nine-month-olds, on the other hand, mastered this problem. Once again, the participants could rely on both binocular and pictorial information about 3D structure.

3.4 Oculomotor Depth and Object Perception: Convergence and Accommodation

Accommodation denotes the adjustment of the eye to bring objects at different distances into sharp focus on the retina. This is achieved by varying the thickness of the lens. *Convergence* denotes the different angles of inclination of the eyes: The eyes swing inwards to focus on a near object and they swing outwards to focus on an object far away.

Even infants under 1 month of age can accommodate in the appropriate direction to targets at various distances (see Aslin, 1993). Similarly, convergent eye movements have been observed in newborns (see Hainline & Riddell, 1996), although younger infants exhibit a great variability in vergence responses (Hainline & Riddell, 1995).

The early presence of accommodation could mean that young infants use this function as a depth cue. Unfortunately, up until today no studies have explored accommodation as a source of depth information. Similarly, there is only sparse evidence for infants' use of convergence as a depth signal. Von Hofsten (1977) has studied reaching behavior in 4- to 7-month-old infants as a function of binocular convergence. According to his results, the infants' reaches were aimed appropriately at the object positions as specified by convergence information. This observation substantiates that by 4 to 7 months of age convergence provides absolute distance information.

Interestingly, previous research has established that both *size constancy* (e.g., Cruikshank, 1941; Day & McKenzie, 1981) and *shape constancy* (e.g., Caron, Caron, & Carlson, 1979; Cook, 1987; Day & McKenzie, 1973) develop within the first months of life. More recent studies have even shown that both constancies are present at birth (Granrud, 1987; Slater, Mattock, & Brown, 1990; Slater & Morison, 1985). In their comment on these findings in newborn babies, Kellman and Arterberry (1998, Chap. 3) conclude that convergence is the most likely source of distance information underlying both abilities. This hypothesis, however, requires further experimental support.

3.5 Pictorial Depth and Object Perception

Even without binocular, kinematic, and oculomotor depth information we are able to see depth and three-dimensional object structure. "Pictorial" or "static-monocular" depth cues have been extensively investigated by Yonas and his colleagues (see Kellman, 1995; Yonas, Arterberry, & Granrud, 1987b). These depth cues are called "pictorial" and "static-monocular," because they make it possible to perceive three-dimensionality in static two-dimensional depictions of 3D scenes and because one eye is sufficient to extract them.

3.5.1 *Pictorial Depth Perception*

The main experimental method employed by Yonas and his colleagues is the "preferential-reaching" technique (see also Brunswik & Cruikshank, 1937). This method is based upon the observation that, from 4 to 5 months of age onwards, when infants are shown two objects they reach for the one that appears to be nearest to them (see Section 3.2.1). Displays in which pictorial cues to depth specified that one object was apparently nearer to the participant than another object are presented to infants under both monocular and binocular viewing conditions. Sensitivity to the pictorial depth information is indicated by more frequent reaches for the object which appears to be nearer, when the infants see the stimulus display monocularly than when they view the scene binocularly. Alternatively, one can compare the reaching behavior of monocularly viewing infants towards a display that contains a pictorially specified depth difference with reaching towards a control display in which no depth order is specified. Again, if the infants display differential reaching behavior towards the display with a depth difference, but not towards the control display, it can be concluded that they are sensitive to the static-monocular depth information.

The studies carried out using the preferential-reaching method demonstrate that 7-month-old infants, but not 5-month-old infants, are able to respond to a variety of pictorial depth cues. More specifically, unlike 5-month-olds, 7-month-old infants are capable of extracting depth from linear perspective, texture gradients, relative size, familiar size, shading, interposition, and surface contour information (e.g., Granrud, Haake, & Yonas, 1985; Granrud & Yonas, 1984; Granrud, Yonas, & Opland, 1985; Kaufmann, Maland, & Yonas, 1981; Yonas, Granrud, Arterberry, & Hanson, 1986; Yonas, Granrud, & Pettersen, 1985; Yonas, Knill, Sen, & Bittinger, 1993). The age trend revealed by these studies has also been confirmed by studies employing a habituation-dishabituation design (Arterberry, Bensen, & Yonas, 1991, Kavšek, 1999; Oross, Francis, Mauk, & Fox, 1987; Yonas & Arterberry, 1994).

Sensitivity to pictorially specified interposition has been investigated by Granrud and Yonas (1984). In this study, both 5- and 7-month-old infants were presented with a coplanar display depicting three overlapping surfaces. If indeed infants perceive the depth stratification within this display, they should grasp at the surface which appears to be nearest to them. Furthermore, there should be no reaching preference for either section of the stimulus if the three segments are separated but have areas identical to those of the interposition display, that is, if any depth order is eliminated from the display. To remove conflicting binocular information, one eye of the participants was covered. The results indicated that the 7-month-old participants reached out significantly more often towards the side of the interposition display which appeared to be nearer than to the same side in the control display. The 5-month-olds' reaching tendencies did not differ significantly between the interposition display and the control display. In a habituation-dishabituation experiment, Yonas and Arterberry (1994, Exp. 2) tested 8-month-olds' ability to distinguish between lines indicating a boundary between two intersecting surfaces, i.e., T-junctions, and lines specifying a surface marking. T-junctions typically occur at the boundary between two overlapping surfaces or 3D objects, that is, they indicate a difference in depth. The crossbar of the T belongs to the occluding surface, the stem of the T is part of the occluded surface (e.g, Guzman, 1968). The infants were habituated to the line drawing of two overlapping rectangles. In addition to T-junctions, the drawing included lines indicating a surface marking. After habituation, the infants saw two test displays, one in which the occluding corner belonging to the front surface had been removed from the habituation stimulus and one in which the surface marking was missing. Results indicated that the participants looked reliably longer at the test display without interposition information. Yonas and Arterberry speculate that by 8 months of age infants are sensitive to T line junction information specifying spatial layout in line drawings. Apparently, the infants react to the disappearance of 3D information rather than responding to the removal of a surface marking.

In a further experiment with 7½- to 8-month-old participants, Yonas and Arterberry (1994, Exp. 1) extended their findings on infants' perception of the spatial meaning of T-junctions to lines indicating edges. "Edges" are tangents of surfaces which are connected but have different orientations in space. The habituation display used was the line drawing of a hexahedron. The stimulus consisted of a Y-junction in the middle and three arrow junctions. Together, these junctions generate the impression of a cubic structure with three visible surfaces. A Y-junction corresponds to a corner formed by three visible surfaces of a body, arrow junctions correspond to a corner formed by two visible surfaces of a body. Furthermore, a marking was drawn on each of the surfaces. In the posthabituation trials, the infants saw two test displays, both of which were derived from the habituation figure. One test display contained only the surface markings and the other one included only the interior edges. The infants significantly preferred the line drawing that contained only the surface markings. This finding suggests that the infants were able to distinguish between surface markings and Y- and arrow junctions that signal edges, as well as being capable of extracting the spatial meaning of these. In a similar study, Kavšek (1999) investigated the pictorial depth cues embedded in the line drawing of a curved object. Specifically, one of the habituation displays was a cylindrical body where the 3D structure was evoked by two curved Y-junctions (see Figure 1a). The combination of two curved Y-junctions corresponds to an edge between two curved surfaces; one of these surfaces is circular, plain, and completely visible, and the other one is vaulted and self-occluding (e.g., Malik, 1987). As soon as the convex edge is omitted, the impression of a line drawing of a spatial body vanishes (Figure 1c). Furthermore, the habituation stimulus had a surface marking. Once again, during the test trials, the participants viewed two displays, one in which the surface marking was deleted from the habituation display (Figure 1b) and one in which the convex edge had been erased (Figure 1c). Eight-month-old infants looked significantly longer at the test display with the edge missing, whereas 5-month-old infants did not. Hence, the older participants behaved as if they were able to extract the spatial meaning of the edge line: When this line is removed, it destroys the impression of being confronted with a spatial object in the picture plane and evokes a significant dishabituation reaction in the infants. Incidentally, all experiments included control groups to rule out the possibility that the infants' visual behavior was determined by spontaneous preferences.

To summarize, by the age of 8 months, infants have developed the ability to use line junctions as a source of information for depth. The question still to be answered is how infants interpret depictions of partially occluded surfaces in the picture plane and line drawings of three-dimensional objects.

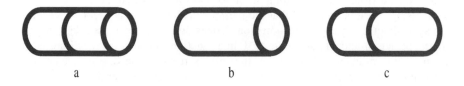

a   b   c

Figure 1. Stimulus displays employed by Kavšek (1999) to study infants' sensitivity to curved Y-junctions (redrawn from Kavšek, 1999).

According to Marr (1982), the internal representation of the environment which is enriched with depth cues, the 2½ D sketch, is viewer-centered rather than object-centered. More specifically, the 2½ D sketch only describes the layout of the visual world from a particular vantage point and does not make the 3D shape of objects explicit. Accordingly, 7- to 8-month-old infants may only perceive static drawings of objects as three-dimensional entities lacking exact shape.

It should be noted, however, that more recent research casts doubt on the observation that sensitivity to pictorial depth cues develops after about 6 months of age. Experiments carried out by Bhatt and his colleagues provided evidence for 3-month-olds' sensitivity to spatial layout when this was indicated by a combination of Y- and arrow junctions (e.g., Bertin & Bhatt, 2002; Bhatt & Bertin, 2001). Furthermore, Kavšek (in press) has shown that 4-month-old female infants responded to the factor of directional alignment of texture elements indicating a spherical surface. In these studies, however, the static-monocular depth cues under investigation are emphasized by embedding them in either a dynamic or a pop-out display which might have a beneficial effect on the infants' performance. Secondly, the young infants' visual performance in these studies might also be based on sensitivity to interruptions in certain proximal stimulus variables. Nevertheless, these findings stress that more research is needed to determine the origin and the development of sensitivity to pictorial depth cues.

3.5.2 Pictorial Object Perception

As has been shown in the previous section, sensitivity to static-monocular depth cues is not present in infants younger than 7 months of age. Furthermore, young infants do not apparently detect static object structure indicated by both pictorial and stereoscopic depth cues (see Section 3.3.2). Positive evidence for the extraction of binocularly specified 3D object structure in 9-month-olds, but not in 6-month-olds, has been reported by Ruff (1978). Consequently, sensitivity to static objects specified by pictorial depth cues can be expected to emerge relatively late.

Indeed, Owsley (1983, Exp. 2) noticed that 4-month-old infants do not react to the difference between a wedge and a cube after habituation to the wedge in a series of stationary orientations. During the habituation trials the infants had only monocular information, whereas in the posthabituation period binocular information was provided. Owsley's findings were later replicated by Kellman (1984) and by Kellman and Short (1987, Exp. 3A). Both the habituation object and the dishabituation objects were depicted two-dimensionally. Kavšek (2001) habituated 7- and 9-month-old infants to the picture of either an elongated cuboid or a cylinder. Spatial orientation of the object varied from habituation trial to habituation trial. Afterwards, the participants had to compare the image of a novel view of the habituation object with that of the other 3D object in the same novel orientation. The 9-month-old participants showed a significant preference for the novel test object, whereas the 7-month-olds exhibited no differential response towards the test displays.

Kavšek's (2001) results parallel the study of Ruff (1978), according to which the ability to extract 3D object structure from multiple static orientations develops after the age of 6 months. However, Kavšek's experiment differs from Ruff's study in that binocular depth information was removed from the stimulus displays. His results therefore imply that discrimination performance in Ruff's study is not necessarily dependent on the presence of binocular depth cues but is also possible even when only static-monocular depth cues are available in the stimulus displays.

All in all, it is apparently easy for infants younger than 6 months of age to reconstruct and encode the geometry of an object from motion and to compare this representation with the spatial structure of a novel object specified by either kinematic or binocular depth cues. On the other hand, the ability to discriminate between two 3D objects after habituation to one of the bodies in multiple static spatial orientations develops after about 7 months of age. It may be difficult for younger infants to construct a mental 3D representation from binocular and/or pictorial depth cues which lasts long enough and is elaborate enough to enable detection of different spatial layouts (see also Kellman, 1996).

The most important class of 3D objects in the infant's visual world are human faces. The full ability to recognize familiar faces and to discriminate between different faces presupposes the combination of a face's internal features into an organized whole as well as an analysis of the face's spatial structure by means of the depth signals available. Up until now, the influence of depth perception on face processing has been neglected. Research is needed that systematically varies both the age of the infants and the mode of stimulus presentation, that is, the kind of depth information which makes the 3D structure of the experimental faces explicit.

Why does sensitivity to the various depth cues emerge in the order outlined in this chapter? Bushnell and Boudreau (1993) argue that development of depth perception is determined by motor development (but see Arterberry, Yonas, & Bensen, 1989; Yonas & Granrud, 1985b). More specifically, motor control of the head may help to discern kinetic depth information, oculomotor control sufficient for accurate vergence of eye movements may permit detection of binocular depth cues, and manual explorative activities with objects may promote extraction of pictorial depth cues.

References

Arditi, A. (1986). Binocular vision. In K. R. Boff, L. Kaufman, & J. P. Thomas (Eds.), *Handbook of perception and human performance* (Vol. 1, pp. 1-41). New York: Wiley.

Arterberry, M. E. (1992). Infants' perception of three-dimensional shape specified by motion-carried information. *Bulletin of the Psychonomic Society, 30*, 337-339.

Arterberry, M. E., Bensen, A. S., & Yonas, A. (1991). Infants' responsiveness to static-monocular depth information: A recovery from habituation approach. *Infant Behavior and Development, 14*, 241-251.

Arterberry, M. E., & Yonas, A. (1988). Infants' sensitivity to kinetic information for three-dimensional object shape. *Perception & Psychophysics, 44*, 1-6.

Arterberry, M. E., Yonas, A., & Bensen, A. S. (1989). Self-produced locomotion and the development of responsiveness to linear perspective and texture gradients. *Developmental Psychology, 25*, 976-982.

Arterberry, M. E., & Yonas, A. (2000). Perception of three-dimensional shape specified by optic flow by 8-week-old infants. *Perception and Psychophysics*, *62*, 550-556.

Aslin, R. N. (1993). Infant accommodation and convergence. In K. Simons (Ed.), *Early visual development. Normal and abnormal* (pp. 30-38). Oxford, UK: Oxford University Press.

Ball, W. A., & Vurpillot, E. (1976). La perception du mouvement en profondeur chez le nourrisson. *Année Psychologique*, *76*, 383-400.

Bertenthal, B. I. (1993). Infants' perception of biomechanical motions: Intrinsic image and knowledge-based constraints. In C. E. Granrud (Ed.), *Visual perception and cognition in infancy. Carnegie Mellon symposia on cognition* (pp. 175-214). Hillsdale, NJ: Erlbaum.

Bertin, E., & Bhatt, R. (2002, April). *Three-month-olds' sensitivity to orientation cues in the 3-D depth plane*. Poster presented at the XIII Biennial International Conference on Infant Studies, Toronto, Ontario, Canada.

Bhatt, R. S., & Bertin, E. (2001). Pictorial cues and three-dimensional information processing in early infancy. *Journal of Experimental Child Psychology*, *80*, 315-332.

Birch, E. E. (1993). Stereopsis in infants and its developmental relation to visual acuity. In K. Simons (Ed.), *Early visual development. Normal and abnormal* (pp. 224-236). Oxford, UK: Oxford University Press.

Braunstein, M. L. (1976). *Depth perception through motion*. New York: Academic Press.

Brunswik, E., & Cruikshank, R. M. (1937). Perceptual size-constancy in early infancy. *Psychological Bulletin*, *34*, 713-714.

Bushnell, E. W., & Boudreau, J. (1993). Motor development and the mind: The potential role of motor abilities as a determinant of aspects of perceptual development. *Child Development*, *64*, 1005-1021.

Caron, A. J., Caron, R. F., & Carlson, V. (1979). Infant perception of the invariant shape of objects varying in slant. *Child Development*, *50*, 716-721.

Cook, M. (1987). The origins of form perception. In B. E. McKenzie & R. H. Day (Eds.), *Perceptual development in early infancy: Problems and issues. Child psychology* (pp. 93-123). Hillsdale, NJ: Erlbaum.

Cook, M., Birch, R., & Griffiths, K. (1986). Discrimination between solid forms in early infancy. *Infant Behavior and Development*, *9*, 189-202.

Craton, L. G., & Yonas, A. (1988). Infants' sensitivity to boundary flow information for depth at an edge. *Child Development*, *59*, 1522-1529.

Cruikshank, R. M. (1941). The development of visual size constancy in early infancy. *The Journal of Genetic Psychology*, *58*, 327-351.

Day, R. H., & McKenzie, B. E. (1973). Perceptual shape constancy in early infancy. *Perception*, *2*, 315-320.

Day, R. H., & McKenzie, B. E. (1981). Infant perception of the invariant size of approaching and receding objects. *Developmental Psychology*, *17*, 670-677.

Eizenman, D. R., & Bertenthal, B. I. (1998). Infants' perception of object unity in translating and rotating displays. *Developmental Psychology*, *34*, 426-434.

Fox, R., Aslin, R. N., Shea, S. L., & Dumais, S. T. (1980). Stereopsis in human infants. *Science*, *207*, 323-324.

Gibson, E. J. (1982). The concept of affordances in development: The renascence of functionalism. In W. A. Collins (Ed.), *The Minnesota symposia on child development. Vol. 15: The concept of development* (pp. 55-81). Hillsdale, NJ: Erlbaum.

Gibson, J. J. (1979). *The ecological approach to visual perception*. Boston: Houghton-Mifflin.

Gillam, B. (1995). The perception of spatial layout from static optical information. In W. Epstein & S. Rogers (Eds.), *Handbook of perception and cognition. Perception of space and motion* (pp. 23-67). San Diego, CA: Academic Press.

Gordon, F. R., & Yonas, A. (1976). Sensitivity to binocular depth information in infants. *Journal of Experimental Child Psychology*, *22*, 413-422.

Granrud, C. E. (1986). Binocular vision and spatial perception on 4- and 5-month-old infants. *Journal of Experimental Psychology: Human Perception and Performance, 12*, 36-49.

Granrud, C. E. (1987). Size constancy in newborn human infants. *Investigative Ophthalmology and Visual Science (Supplement), 28*, 5.

Granrud, C. E., Haake, R. J., & Yonas, A. (1985). Infants' sensitivity to familiar size: The effect of memory on spatial perception. *Perception & Psychophysics, 37*, 459-466.

Granrud, C. E., & Yonas, A. (1984). Infants' perception of pictorially specified interposition. *Journal of Experimental Child Psychology, 37*, 500-511.

Granrud, C. E., Yonas, A., & Opland, E. A. (1985). Infants' sensitivity to the depth cue of shading. *Perception & Psychophysics, 37*, 415-419.

Granrud, C. E., Yonas, A., Smith, I. M. , Arterberry, M. E., Glicksman, M. L., & Sorknes, A. C. (1984). Infants' sensitivity to accretion and deletion of texture as information for depth at an edge. *Child Development, 55*, 1630-1636.

Guzman, A. (1968). Decomposition of a visual scene into three-dimensional bodies. *AFIPS Proceedings of the Fall Joint Computer Conference, 33*, 291-304.

Hainline, L., & Riddell, P. M. (1995). Binocular alignment and vergence in early infancy. *Vision Research, 35*, 3229-3236.

Hainline, L., & Riddell, P. M. (1996). Eye alignment and convergence in young infants. In F. Vital-Durand, J. Atkinson, & O. J. Braddick (Eds.), *Infant vision* (pp. 221-247). Oxford, UK: Oxford University Press.

Hochberg, J. (1971). Perception: II. Space and movement. In J. W. Kling & L. A. Riggs (Eds.), *Woodworth and Schlosberg's experimental psychology* (pp. 475-550). New York: Holt, Rinehart & Winston.

Johansson, G. (1970). On theories for visual space perception. *Scandinavian Journal of Psychology, 11*, 67-74.

Johnson, S. P., & Aslin, R. N. (1995). Perception of object unity in 2-month-old infants. *Developmental Psychology, 31*, 739-745.

Johnson, S. P., & Mason, U. (2002). Perception of kinetic illusory contours by two-month-old infants. *Child Development, 73*, 22-34.

Jouen, F., & Lepecq, J. C. (1989). La sensibilité au flux optique chez le nouveau-né. *Psychologie Francaise, 34*, 13-18.

Kaufmann, R., Maland, J., & Yonas, A. (1981). Sensitivity of 5- and 7-month-old infants to pictorial depth information. *Journal of Experimental Child Psychology, 32*, 162-168.

Kaufmann-Hayoz, R., Kaufmann, F., & Stucki, M. (1986). Kinetic contours in infants' visual perception. *Child Development, 57*, 292-299.

Kavšek, M. J. (1999). Infants' responsiveness to line junctions in curved objects. *Journal of Experimental Child Psychology, 72*, 177-192.

Kavšek, M. J. (2001). Infant perception of static three-dimensional form: The contribution of pictorial depth cues. *Cognitive Processes, 2*, 199-213.

Kavšek, M. J. (in press). Infants' perception of directional alignment of texture elements on a spherical surface. *Infant and Child Development*.

Kellman, P. J. (1984). Perception of three-dimensional form by human infants. *Perception & Psychophysics, 36*, 353-358.

Kellman, P. J. (1993). Kinematic foundations of infant visual perception. In C. E. Granrud (Ed.), *Visual perception and cognition in infancy* (pp. 121-173). Hillsdale, NJ: Erlbaum.

Kellman, P. J. (1995). Ontogenesis of space and motion perception. In W. Epstein & S. Rogers (Eds.), *Handbook of perception and cognition. Perception of space and motion* (pp. 327-364). San Diego, CA: Academic Press.

Kellman, P. J. (1996). The origins of object perception. In R. Gelman & T. Kit-Fong Au (Eds.), *Perceptual and cognitive development. Handbook of perception and cognition (2nd ed.)* (pp. 3-48). San Diego, CA: Academic Press.

Kellman, P. J., & Arterberry, M. E. (1998). *The cradle of knowledge.* Cambridge, MA: MIT Press.

Kellman, P. J., & Short, K. R. (1987). Development of three-dimensional form perception. *Journal of Experimental Psychology: Human Perception and Performance*, *13*, 545-557.

Kellman, P. J., & Spelke, E. S. (1983). Perception of partly occluded objects in infancy. *Cognitive Psychology*, *15*, 483-524.

Kellman, P. J., von Hofsten, C., & Soares, J. (1987). Concurrent motion in infant event perception. *Infant Behavior and Development*, *10*, 1-10.

Malik, J. (1987). Interpreting line drawings of curved objects. *International Journal of Computer Vision*, *1*, 73-103.

Marr, D. (1982). Vision: A computational investigation into the human representation and processing of visual information. San Francisco: Freeman.

Náñez, J. E., & Yonas, A. (1994). Effects of luminance and texture motion on infant defensive reactions to optical collision. *Infant Behavior and Development*, *17*, 165-174.

Oross, S., Francis, E., Mauk, D., & Fox, R. (1987). The Ames window illusion: Perception of illusory motion by human infants. *Journal of Experimental Psychology: Human Perception and Performance*, *13*, 609-613.

Owsley, C. (1983). The role of motion in infants' perception of solid shape. *Perception*, *12*, 707-717.

Ruff, H. A. (1978). Infant recognition of the invariant form of objects. *Child Development*, *49*, 293-306.

Schmuckler, M. A., & Li, N. S. (1998). Looming responses to obstacles and apertures: The role of accretion and deletion of background texture. *Psychological Science*, *9*, 49-52.

Schmuckler, M. A., & Proffitt, D. R. (1994). Infants' perception of kinetic depth and stereokinetic displays. *Journal of Experimental Psychology: Human Perception and Performance*, *20*, 122-130.

Shaw, L., Roder, B., & Bushnell, E. W. (1986). Infants' identification of three-dimensional form from transformations of linear perspective. *Perception & Psychophysics*, *40*, 301-310.

Slater, A., Mattock, A., & Brown, E. (1990). Size constancy at birth: Newborn infants' responses to retinal and real size. *Journal of Experimental Child Psychology*, *49*, 314-322.

Slater, A., & Morison, V. (1985). Shape constancy and slant perception at birth. *Perception*, *14*, 337-344.

Spitz, R. V., Stiles, J., & Siegel, R. M. (1993). Infant use of relative motion as information for form: Evidence for spatiotemporal integration of complex motion displays. *Perception & Psychophysics*, *53*, 190-199.

Ullman, S. (1979). *The interpretation of visual motion*. Cambridge, MA: MIT Press.

von Hofsten, C. (1977). Binocular convergence as a determinant of reaching behavior in infancy. *Perception*, *6*, 139-144.

von Hofsten, C., Kellman, P., & Putaansuu, J. (1992). Young infants' sensitivity to motion parallax. *Infant Behavior and Development*, *15*, 245-264.

Walker, A. S., Owsley, C. J., Megaw-Nyce, J., Gibson, E. J., & Bahrick, L. B. (1980). Detection of elasticity as an invariant property of objects by young infants. *Perception*, *9*, 713-718.

Yonas, A., & Arterberry, M. E. (1994). Infants perceive spatial structure specified by line junctions. *Perception*, *23*, 1427-1435.

Yonas, A., Arterberry, M. E., & Granrud, C. E. (1987a). Four-month-old infants' sensitivity to binocular and kinetic information for three-dimensional object shape. *Child Development*, *58*, 910-917.

Yonas, A., Arterberry, M. E., & Granrud, C. E. (1987b). Space perception in infancy. *Annals of Child Development*, *4*, 1-34.

Yonas, A., & Granrud, C. E. (1985a). Reaching as a measure of infants' spatial perception. In G. Gottlieb & N. A. Krasnegor (Eds.), *Measurement of audition and vision in the first year of postnatal life: A methodological overview*. (pp. 301-322). Norwood, NJ: Ablex.

Yonas, A., & Granrud, C. E. (1985b). The development of sensitivity to kinetic, binocular and pictorial depth information in human infants. In D. J. Ingle, M. Jeannerod, & D. N. Lee (Eds.), *Brain mechanisms and spatial vision*. (pp. 113-145). Dordrecht, The Netherlands: Nijhoff.

Yonas, A., Granrud, C. E., Arterberry, M. E., & Hanson, B. L. (1986). Infants' distance perception from linear perspective and texture gradients. *Infant Behavior and Development, 9*, 247-256.

Yonas, A., Granrud, C. E., & Pettersen, L. (1985). Infants' sensitivity to relative size information for distance. *Developmental Psychology, 21*, 161-167.

Yonas, A., & Hartman, B. (1993). Perceiving the affordance of contact in four- and five-month-old infants. *Child Development, 64*, 298-308.

Yonas, A., Knill, D.C., Sen, M., & Bittinger, K. A. (1993). The development in human infants of sensitivity to surface contour information for 3-D layout. In S. Valenti & J. Pittenger (Eds.), *Studies in perception and action II. Posters presented in the VIIth International conference on event perception and action* (pp. 166-177). Hillsdale, NJ: Erlbaum.

Yonas, A., & Pick, H. L. (1975). An approach to the study of infant space perception. In L. B. Cohen & P. Salapatek (Eds.), *Infant Perception: From Sensation to Cognition. Vol. II: Perception of space, speech, and sound* (pp. 3-31). New York: Academic Press.

Address for Correspondence

Michael Kavšek
University of Bonn
Department of Psychology
Römerstr. 164
D-53117 Bonn
Germany
E-mail: kavsek@uni-bonn.de

Part II:
Face Processing from Infancy to Adulthood

4

Face Processing During the First Decade of Life

Gudrun Schwarzer

Nicola Zauner

Monika Korell

4.1 Introduction

Face processing has an impressive start in early infancy. Nine minutes after birth, newborns already prefer faces to other visual patterns and prefer to look at a face-like pattern rather than at a scrambled face (Goren, Sarty, & Wu, 1975; Johnson, Dziurawiec, Ellis, & Morton, 1991; Valenza, Simion, Macchi, Cassia, & Umilta, 1996). Two hypotheses have been put forward to explain newborns' early preference for faces. According to the so-called "structural hypothesis," advanced by Johnson and Morton (1991), infants direct their attention to faces right after birth due to an inborn reflex-like mechanism ("conspec"). This mechanism is effective during the first two months of life and contains an inborn representation of the human face, including information about the spatial distribution of the main elements of the face.

An explanation competing with the structural hypothesis is the so-called "sensoric hypothesis" (Banks & Salapatek, 1981; Kleiner, 1987; Kleiner & Banks, 1987), which assumes that newborns' early preference for faces can be explained without recourse to an inborn knowledge of faces. Here it is argued that faces are preferred by newborns because the physical properties of the visual pattern of faces, unlike other visual patterns, are perfectly matched to the sensoric abilities of newborns. Therefore, compared to other visual stimuli, faces are extremely interesting and informative for newborns. However, in a series of experiments Valenza, Simion, Macchi, Cassia, and Umilta (1996) tested how far the structural information of faces and the distribution of spatial frequencies in faces play a role in the preference for faces. They showed that even if the distribution of spatial frequencies is optimal for infants' sensoric abilities, their preference for faces was determined by the structural information of the faces. This may lead to the conclusion, as implied by the structural hypothesis, that an inborn representation of the specific structure of the face exists that is responsible for the early preference for faces observed in newborns.

Whereas the inborn representation of the structure of faces enables young infants to detect faces in their surroundings, it is assumed that this is not sufficient to help them differentiate individual faces. To do this, young babies require experience with faces and learning. Until now, however, it is still not fully understood which modes of processing young infants use to distinguish between different faces. Taking into account that young infants' visual acuity is poor in comparison to adults, this might lead them to process more global and configural information of faces rather than individual features (Chapter 1). As far as older infants are concerned whose visual acuity works relatively well, it is still unclear whether they learn to distinguish faces by processing them analytically (on the basis of single features) or configurally on the basis of a configuration of facial features. This question is addressed in the first part of this chapter. The second part of the chapter examines to what extent the nature of face processing changes during subsequent development from the age of 2 to 10 years.

4.2 Face Processing in Infancy

4.2.1 Previous Studies About Face Processing in Infancy

Most studies on face processing in infancy examined different modes of processing in a rather indirect way. For example, Deruelle and de Schoenen (1991) showed that the right hemisphere was unable to process a schematic face analytically, component by component, whereas the left hemisphere was able to process the faces in this way. Moreover, Kestenbaum and Nelson (1990) examined how different processing modes support the discrimination of facial expressions in infancy. They examined the degree to which 7-month-old infants were able to discriminate facial expressions of happiness, fear, and anger in upright and inverted orientations. If the task required the categorization of facial expressions over changing identities – in other words, if the task required infants to focus on more than one single feature – infants were able to discriminate between the expressions only when the faces were shown in an upright position. However, if the task was simplified so that a discrimination on the basis of one single feature was possible, infants were able to discriminate between the facial expressions in both upright and inverted orientations. In this case, the processing mode was not affected by the orientation of the faces. Thus, even young infants were able to process facial expressions both on the basis of single features (analytically) and on the basis of more configural information. However, it seemed that as soon as only a single feature was available, they preferred the analytical processing mode.

A study carried out by Slater, Quinn, Hayes, and Brown (2000) on infants' understanding of facial attractiveness can also be interpreted with reference to the question of analytical and configural processing. Slater et al. were interested in whether there is an inborn preference for attractive faces over unattractive faces. They showed newborns different pairs of faces, each consisting of an attractive and an unattractive face, in a preferential looking task. It was found that the babies preferred the attractive faces when the stimuli were presented in an upright position but not when they were inverted. One interpretation of the different response to the attractiveness of upright and inverted faces is that the babies responded to some kind of configural information in the upright condition. Since this configural information is usually lost when the faces are inverted (e.g., Yin, 1969), they no longer responded to the inverted faces. Thus, this study provides hints about infants' ability to process faces configurally.

In all, there are only a very few studies that have tested infants' analytical and configural modes of face processing in a more direct way. Cohen and Cashon (2001) investigated 7-month-old infants by using the so-called "switch design." This design made it possible to examine whether the infants respond to one or more independent features of faces (analytical processing) or to a configuration of facial features. First, the authors habituated the infants to two adult female faces. Then, the infants were tested with a familiar habituation face, a "switch face" and a novel face. The switch face was a composite of the two habituation faces, consisting of the internal section of one face and the external section of the other face. Half the infants saw the faces in an upright, the other half in an inverted position. The authors found that in the upright condition the infants looked longer at the "switch test face" than at the familiar test face. In the inverted condition, the infants did not look longer at the switch test face; they only looked longer at the novel test face. Cohen and Cashon (2001) argue that, since all the features of the switch face are familiar to the infants after habituation, if they do not look longer at the switch face than at the familiar face, they must be responding to the internal and external sections of the faces independently of each other (analytically). On the other hand, if they do look longer at the switch face, this must be because they are responding to the new configuration of the internal and external sections of the faces. Thus, with respect to their data, the authors conclude that 7-month-old infants process the configuration of the internal and external sections of the faces when the faces are upright, whereas they process the sections independently of each other when the faces are inverted (see also Younger, 1992).

However, as Cohen and Cashon (2001) only combined the internal section as a whole with the external section of the faces, it is not clear from their study if the infants were combining all or only some subset of internal and external features. It *is* clear from a study by Slater, Bremner, Johnson, Sherwood, Hayes, and Brown (2000) that newborn infants distinguish two dimensional depictions of faces on the basis of all the internal features. The authors showed that the infants preferred to look at attractive faces on the basis of internal features only. It has still not been clarified just how infants process the internal section of faces, the section that is usually called face, i.e., whether they process the facial features independently of each other (analytically) or configurally. To resolve this question, our own studies (Schwarzer & Zauner, 2002) used the switch design but we switched four single facial features (eyes, nose, mouth, facial contour). We habituated 8-month-old infants to the two schematically drawn faces (child and adult face) as shown in Table 1.

The subsequent test phase consisted of 3 different conditions (switch, novel, and familiar). In the "switch condition," we presented a switch face where a single feature of one of the habituation faces (either eyes, nose, mouth or facial contour) had been replaced by the corresponding feature of the other habituation face (see Table 1), e.g., the adult eyes were inserted into the child face and vice versa. Before running the main experiment, it was shown in 8 single control studies that 8-month-old infants were able to distinguish between the habituation faces and the corresponding switch faces, i.e., they were able to perceive the differences between the child habituation face and each of the switch faces containing an adult feature (switch faces in the top line of Table 1), and between the adult habituation face and the switch faces containing a child feature (switch faces in the second line of Table 1).

If infants processed single features of the faces during the habituation phase of the main experiment, we did not expect them to dishabituate to the switch faces in the test phase, since the features of the switch faces were already familiar to them. If, however, the infants processed the faces configurally in the habituation phase, we expected there to be an increase in looking time when the switch face was presented, due to the new facial configuration.

In the "novel condition," the infants also received the child and adult habituation faces in the habituation phase, but instead of a switch face they were shown a completely new face in the test phase (see novel face in Table 1). In this case, we expected the children to dishabituate to the test face because this face contained new facial features as well as a new facial configuration. In the "familiar condition," infants again were first habituated to the adult and child habituation faces and then shown the child or adult habituation face in the test phase. In this condition, an increase in looking time in the test phase was not expected. This condition should rule out the possibility that looking times increase in the test phase due to natural fluctuation. Figure 1 shows the findings of our study in terms of looking times.

Table 1. Facial stimuli used in the experiment on infants' modes of face processing.

Habituation Faces (child face/ adult face)	Test Faces Switch Eyes	Test Faces Switch Nose	Test Faces Switch Mouth	Test Faces Switch Facial Contour	Novel Face

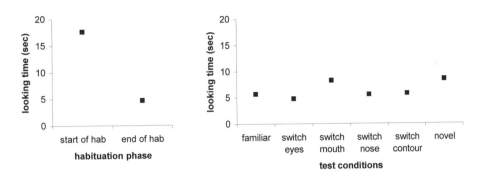

Figure 1. Mean looking times of 8-month-old infants for habituation phase and test conditions are shown individually. Independent samples participated in the different test conditions.

When eyes, nose or contour of a face were switched in the test phase, the infants showed no increase in looking time. If, however, the mouth was switched, they fixated the face significantly longer than each of the familiar faces. As expected, infants dishabituated to the novel face and not to the familiar face. Thus, our results show that the mode of processing depends on the feature that is varied in the face. Eyes, nose, and facial contour were processed independently of the facial context (analytically), whereas the mouth was processed in conjunction with the facial context (configurally). In order to rule out the possibility that these findings were due to the faces being presented as schematic stimuli, we carried out a similar experiment using more natural looking faces. In this study, the early integration of the mouth into the face was also observed in 8-month-old infants.

To learn more about the development of face processing during the first year of life, the switch design already described was used to study how younger infants (4- and 6-month-olds) processed the schematically drawn faces shown above (Zauner & Schwarzer, 2002). The findings showed that the 4- to 6-month-old infants did not dishabituate to the different switch faces and the familiar face, but did dishabituate to the novel face. Thus, they showed the characteristic pattern of analytical processing. Therefore, with regard to face processing during the first year of life, we conclude that 4- to 6-month-old infants process faces analytically, whereas 8-month-old infants process facial features both analytically and configurally.

4.2.2 Conclusions About Face Processing in Infancy

Our findings indicate that face processing in infancy depends on the age of the child and on the facial feature to be processed. The eyes are processed analytically, independently of the context of the whole face between 4 and 8 months of age. The mouth is also processed analytically by 4- to 6-month-olds, but by the age of 8 months it is processed configurally.

Why does the mouth play such a special role in face processing in infancy? It could be that the mouth is more important than other facial features and that infants' attention is, therefore, drawn to this feature from an early age, particularly as the mouth is in constant movement when we smile, laugh, and talk; and infants, as is known, react to movement (see Kellman & Arterberry, 1998). Imitation studies have shown that newborns pay great attention to the mouth movements of adults and are able to imitate these (e.g., Meltzoff & Moore, 1977; Meltzoff & Moore, 1994). Infants also express themselves to a great extent via their mouth, i.e., by crying, sucking, yawning etc. Also, the mouth is important for communication and the intake of food. For these reasons, infants may focus on the mouth more intensely than on the other features when they perceive faces and they may notice that changes of the mouth also cause changes of other features. This in turn may lead infants to integrate the mouth into the face by an earlier age than other facial features.

Taking the results of Cohen and Cashon's study (2001) and those of our own work together, the following conclusions about face processing in infancy can be drawn. Cohen and Cashon (2001) showed that 7-month-old infants process faces configurally when both the interior and exterior of the faces had been exchanged. Our studies showed how infants process the internal section of the face. We could show that 8-month-old infants had already built up a configuration between the mouth and the face whereas this was not the case with regard to the eyes, nose, and facial contour. Moreover, our study revealed changes in the development of face processing during the first 8 months of life. It could be shown that 4- to 6-month-old infants process features such as the eyes and mouth analytically, still independently of the face as a whole, whereas 8-month-olds process the mouth in conjunction with the whole face, configurally. Thus, depending on the facial feature, there seems to be a developmental shift from analytical to configural face processing during the first year of life – at least for the processing of schematic faces. To what extent these modes of processing change in subsequent years will be described in another section of this chapter (see also Carey & Diamond, 1994; Tanaka, Kay, Grinnell, Stansfield, & Szechter, 1998).

This change from analytical to configural face processing during the first year of life is partly in line with the general approach to information processing as developed by Cohen (1998). Cohen assumes that up to the age of 5 months, infants process only single features of objects (analytical processing) and that it is only between 5 and 7 months of age that infants integrate these single features into a perception of the entire object (configural processing). With respect to the feature "mouth," our findings confirm the assumption that 8-month-old infants process the mouth in the context of the entire face. With regard to how the eyes were processed, no course of development could be observed. Presumably, only older infants integrate the eyes into the face. It thus seems that the validity of Cohen's approach (1998) depends on the facial feature in question.

Altogether, it is possible to draw parallels between our findings and those studies on face processing in infancy in which the role of analytical and configural processes have been studied indirectly. Deruelle and de Schoenen (1991), for example, studied hemispheric participation during face processing in infancy and showed that 4- and 9-month-old infants seem to process faces analytically (via the left hemisphere) and configurally (via the right hemisphere). Kestenbaum and Nelson (1990) also emphasize analytical and configural processing when infants categorize facial expressions. Similar to our results obtained on 8-month-old infants, it could be shown that the use of one mode of processing (analytical or configural) does not mean that the other is not available. Instead, in older infants the conditions (e.g., upright or inverted condition, switched eyes, nose, mouth or facial contour in the present study) determine whether the analytical or configural mode of processing is accessed.

4.3 Face Processing in Childhood

Despite the fact that infants already have impressive face identification abilities during infancy, face recognition continues to undergo development during the first decade of life. Young children have more difficulty than adults when encoding and subsequently identifying unfamiliar faces. Marked improvement between the ages of 2 and 10 is observed on simple recognition tasks. One explanation for these age-related differences in face recognition could be differences in the modes of face processing within this age range.

In the following section, we will present research concerning the development of analytical and configural modes of face processing in the 6- to 10-year-old age-range which allows a comparison with the infant research described above. In the subsequent sections we will present developmental changes in the 2- to 10-year-old age-range with regard to analytical and holistic processing modes. In a further section of the chapter we will show to what extent analytical and holistic processing modes are associated with face recognition performance in different age groups. In the holistic processing mode as opposed to the configural mode of face processing, relations between faces in terms of overall similarity are emphasized. This definition of holistic processing goes back to Garner's (1974) characterization of integral stimuli. Overall similarity relations are holistic insofar as "the stimulus representations that are accessed in processing are accessed as wholes, rather than as a concatenation of independent properties...When stimuli are compared, they are compared as wholes and the relation that is internally computed is their overall similarity. These holistic representations are not decomposed while doing computations and arriving at a response during the processing episode" (Kemler Nelson, 1989, p. 374).

4.3.1 Analytical and Configural Modes of Face Processing in 6- to 10-Year-Old Children

Studies on the development of analytical and configural processing in older children are different from the infant studies mentioned above with respect to the methodology applied. The use of different methods with older children is inevitable, however, as they are too active physically and cognitively to participate in habituation and dishabituation studies.

Research carried out by Carey and Diamond (1994) which studied face processing in 6- to 10-year-old children employed a method that most closely resembles the logic behind the switch design used in our study to examine analytical and configural processing in infancy. Using the task of Young, Hellawell, and Hay (1987), Carey and Diamond (1994) asked the children to name the upper half of a face while the lower half of the face belonged to a different person. In different conditions, the face halves were aligned (composite faces) or not aligned (non-composite faces) and the faces were shown upright or inverted. The authors report that the responses of the children were only slowed down by the mismatch of the upper half of the composite faces compared to the non-composite faces when the faces were upright. The results showed that 6- to 10-year-old children process one half of the face, i.e., the upper half, in connection with its complement, the lower half. The upper half of the face is thus perceived and processed configurally in conjunction with the lower half.

Research carried out by Tanaka, Kay, Grinnell, Stansfield, and Szechter (1998) also points in this direction. In their task, 6- to 10-year-old children were asked to memorize faces together with their respective names. After this learning period, they were shown the single parts of the memorized faces, the parts being either shown in the context of the whole face or in isolation, i.e., without the facial context. The children were then asked to name the facial parts presented within a face or in isolation. The study revealed that children of all age groups were more successful at identifying parts of faces when these were shown in the context of the whole face than when they were shown in isolation. Thus, facial context is important for the recall of simple facial features at 6 to 10 years of age. This in turn means that children of this age range are sensitive to a change in facial configuration.

Thus, the results on face processing in 6- to 10-year-olds are congruent with our results (Schwarzer & Zauner, 2002) on face processing in infancy. In our studies we have shown that 8-month-old babies have already begun to respond to changes in facial configuration, i.e., that they have started to integrate the facial features (the mouth) at 8 months into the face. According to the studies of Carey and Diamond (1994) and Tanaka et al. (1998), by the age of 6 years, children seem to have completely integrated the face halves and the various facial features into the face.

4.3.2 Analytical and Holistic Modes of Face Processing in 2- to 10-Year-Old Children

Encouraged by studies within the field of general developmental psychology on analytical and holistic processing of visual stimuli other than faces (Ward, 1989 for an overview), we carried out a series of studies on the development of these modes of processing in the domain of face processing (Schwarzer, 2000). In contrast to the studies mentioned above, our studies were concerned with holistic processing in comparison with analytical processing. Here, holistic processing of faces is defined as the comparison of faces in terms of their overall similarity.

To examine holistic face processing in terms of overall similarity and analytical face processing (focusing on single facial features), we used a categorization task in our studies. Children aged between 6 and 10 years and, for purposes of comparison, adults learned via feedback to classify 8 schematically drawn faces into two categories (learning phase). These faces had been derived from the child and adult faces used in the infant studies described above (see Schwarzer, 2000 for details). Two independent and randomly selected groups of each age were shown the faces of the two categories in either an upright or an inverted position. Since the facial categories were based on a family resemblance structure, the learning process could have analytical character (focusing on one of the single features, namely eyes, nose, mouth, or facial contour) or holistic character (based on the overall similarity of the faces). Following the learning phase, 8 test faces were presented in two random orders (2 x 8 faces). As in the learning phase, the children's task was to categorize the faces. By analyzing the categorization patterns for the test faces, it was possible to determine the processing strategy for each of the participants. The general basis of the diagnosis of an analytical processing mode was that at least 14 out of the 16 test faces were processed by focusing on the same facial feature (eyes, nose, mouth, or facial contour). For the diagnosis of the holistic processing mode, here too at least 14 out of the 16 test faces had to be categorized based on overall similarity.

As can be seen in Figure 2, the 6- to 7-year-olds categorized both the upright and the inverted faces almost completely analytically, whereas the 10-year-olds made comparatively more holistic judgments in the upright condition. In the adult group, a clear effect of inversion on the modes of processing could be observed. Adults almost always processed upright faces holistically and inverted faces analytically. The participants of the group "other" in the different age groups also focused on single facial attributes but did not use the same attribute consistently. Thus, the results of this study show both a developmental trend from analytical to holistic processing and an effect of inversion during development in terms of qualitatively different modes of processing upright and inverted faces.

To fill the gap between research on face processing in infancy and children above the age of 6, we presented the categorization task described above to children between 2 and 5 years of age (Schwarzer & Korell, 2001; Schwarzer, 2002). To this end, the task was made suitable for children without, however, changing the general setup of the experiment.

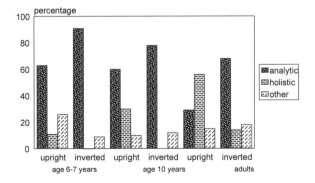

Figure 2. Percentage of processing modes in the categorization of upright and inverted faces in 6- to 10-year-old children and adults.

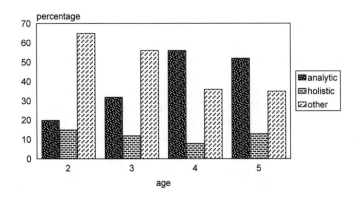

Figure 3. Percentage of processing modes in 2- to 5-year-old children.

As depicted in Figure 3, the majority of the 2-year-olds categorized the faces by focusing inconsistently on different facial features (using the strategy "other"), whereas the majority of the 5-year-olds focused consistently on one single facial feature (using the strategy "analytic"). Thus, analytical processing increased with age and the strategy "other" decreased with age. Holistic processing, however, remained almost constant. It was only shown by a minority of children in each age group.

All in all, studies on children of 2 to 10 years of age illustrate that 2- to 3-year-old children mainly analyze single facial features, thereby still focusing alternately on different facial features. By the age of 5, a consistent focus on a specific facial feature has been established. From this age onwards, a continuous increase in holistic processing can be observed which is accompanied by a decrease in analytical processing. In adults, eventually, holistic processing is the predominant mode of processing. Thus, over the course of development, there is a shift from an analytical to a holistic processing of faces.

4.3.3 Correspondence Between the Analytical and Holistic Modes of Face Processing and Face Recognition Performance

The studies by Carey and Diamond (1994) and Tanaka et al. (1998) mentioned above examined analytical and configural processing with regard to the question of whether the identification of the upper half of the face or the recognition of face parts is influenced by the context of the entire face. Both studies show that already from the age of 6 years onwards, the face as a whole exerts an influence on the perception of its parts. In our own work (Schwarzer, 2000, 2002; Schwarzer & Korell, 2001), we examined the analytical and holistic modes of processing. Instead of measuring recognition and identification performance we measured category assignment. Children of different ages were asked to categorize faces. They could either focus on a single feature (analytical processing) or on the overall similarity of faces (holistic processing). As described above, young children aged between 2 and 7 years focus on single features when categorizing faces and hence proceed in an analytical way. Older children and adults, on the other hand, increasingly show a holistic mode of categorization and take the whole face into account. However, as our studies examined analytical and holistic face processing in the context of a categorization task, it is still unclear as to whether mode of categorization and face recognition performance correspond. Therefore, we explicitly studied what kind of recognition performance is associated with the analytical and holistic categorization of faces (Groß & Schwarzer, 2002).

The categorization task and a recognition task were given to 7- to 11-year-old children. The categorization task consisted of the learning and test phase described above. In the recognition task, the children were shown the 8 test faces of the categorization task and 16 new schematically drawn distractor faces. The participants were asked whether they knew the individual faces shown to them or not. Thus it was possible to determine an analytical or holistic mode of face processing for each participant from the categorization task, and face recognition performance could be analyzed on the basis of the recognition task. Beyond that, the relationship could be established between both types of data, that is, between mode of processing and recognition performance.

Whereas in 7- to 8-year-old children analytical and holistic processing are accompanied by similar recognition performance, with increasing age holistic processing has a clear advantage over the analytical mode (see Figure 4).

Adults showed a significantly better recognition performance when processing faces in the mode predominant in their age group, that is, holistically. Interestingly, in the youngest age group, the inconsistent analysis ("other") is, if compared to analytical and holistic processing, associated with the best recognition performance for that age. Thus, there was an age specific relationship between processing mode and face recognition performance. In children, the inconsistent analytical processing mode led to best face recognition performance whereas in adults, best face recognition performance was associated with holistic processing.

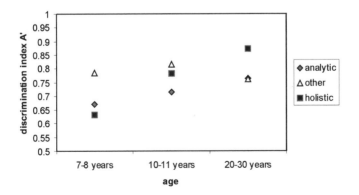

Figure 4. Correspondence between modes of face processing and recognition performance (calculated as the ability to discriminate targets from distractors) in 7- to 11-year-old children and adults.

4.4 Conclusion

The research presented here indicates that 4-month-old infants process single features of schematically-drawn faces such as the eyes and mouth analytically, that is, independently of information provided by other characteristics of the face. Then, with increasing age, single features gradually become integrated into the face and therefore babies start to respond to changes in the facial configuration. Studies conducted by our research group showed that 8-month-old infants process the mouth in conjunction with the whole face. Cohen and Cashon (2001) also follow this line of research by emphasizing configural processing of the interior and exterior of the face.

Carey and Diamond (1994) and Tanaka et al. (1998) studied older children with the aim of finding out whether they respond to changes in the facial configuration. They showed that by the age of 6, children are sensitive to changes in the facial configuration and that the single features have been completely integrated into the face. These studies on face processing in infancy and in older children thus suggest that with increasing age, a shift occurs away from the independent, context-free analytical processing of single facial features in early infancy (4 to 6 months) towards configural processing and the full integration of all single features into the face.

If analytical and holistic modes of processing are studied when faces are categorized, further changes become apparent with increasing age. Between 2 and 7 years of age, children mainly categorize faces analytically on the basis of single features, both consistently and inconsistently. With increasing age, face categorization gradually becomes more holistic, i.e., becomes based on the overall similarity of the face. Thus a shift can also be observed from analytical to holistic processing within the context of face categorization. Most strikingly, holistic face processing can only be found in the adult group associated with the best face recognition performance. By contrast, in children the analytical (inconsistent) processing strategy leads to the best face recognition performance. Thus, the correspondence between mode of face processing and face recognition performance differs in children and adults.

All in all, the empirical evidence clearly indicates that during the first decade of life single facial features gradually become integrated into the face and that, with increasing age, the entire face is accessed more and more frequently for the purpose of categorization. Provided that infants' visual acuity has reached an adequate level, it can be concluded that both processing modes, configural and holistic processing, develop from analytical processing. One explanation for the importance of analytical face processing could be the characteristics of the child's information processing system since this is not yet fully developed. For example, processing capacity increases dramatically during the first years of life. Low processing capacity may be better matched to the processing of single facial features than to configural or holistic processing. Another reason could be the increasing amount of facial representations. This could lead children to discover that configural or holistic information about a face is the optimal information to enable differentiation between the huge variety of faces. One aim of future studies should be to shed more light on age-specific factors of children's information processing that could influence their face processing.

References

Banks, M. S., & Salapatek, P. (1981). Infant pattern vision: A new approach based on the contrast sensitivity function. *Journal of Experimental Child Psychology, 31,* 1-45.

Carey, S., & Diamond, R. (1994). Are faces perceived as configurations more by adults than by children? *Visual Cognition, 1,* 253-274.

Cohen, L. B. (1998). An information-processing approach to infant perception and cognition. In F. Simion & G. Butterworth (Eds.), *The development of sensory, motor, and cognitive capacities in early infancy* (pp. 277-300). Hove, UK: Psychology Press.

Cohen, L. B., & Cashon, C. H. (2001). Do 7-month-old infants process independent features or facial configurations? *Infant and Child Development, 10,* 83-92.

Deruelle, C., & de Schoenen, S. (1991). Hemispheric asymmetries in visual pattern processing in infancy. *Brain and Cognition, 16,* 151-179.

Garner, W. R. (1974). *The processing of information and structure.* Hillsdale, NJ: Erlbaum.

Goren, C. C., Sarty, M., & Wu, P. J. K. (1975). Visual following and pattern discrimination of face-like stimuli by newborn infants. *Pediatrics, 56,* 544-549.

Groß, C. & Schwarzer, G. (2002). Wiedererkennung von Gesichtern im Entwicklungs-verlauf: Welche Rolle spielt der Verarbeitungsmodus? E. van der Meer, H. Hagendorf, R. Beyer, F. Krüger, A. Nuthmann & S. Schulz (Eds.), *43. Kongress der Deutschen Gesellschaft für Psychologie.* Lengerich, Germany: Pabst Science Publishers.

Johnson, M. H., Dziurawiec, S., Ellis, H., & Morton, J. (1991). Newborns' preferential tracking of face-like stimuli and its subsequent decline. *Cognition, 40,* 1-19.

Johnson, M. H., & Morton, J. (1991). *Biology and cognitive development: The case of face recognition.* Oxford, UK: Blackwell.

Kellman, P. J., & Arterberry, M.E. (1998). *The cradle of knowledge: Development of perception in infancy.* Cambridge, MA: MIT Press.

Kemler Nelson, D. G. (1989). The nature and occurrence of holistic processing. In B. E. Shepp & S. Ballesteros (Eds.), *Object perception: Structure and process* (pp. 357-386). Hillsdale, NJ: Erlbaum.

Kestenbaum, R., & Nelson, C. A. (1990). The recognition and categorization of upright and inverted emotional expressions by 7-month-old infants. *Infant Behavior and Development, 13,* 497-511.

Kleiner, K. A. (1987). Amplitude and phase spectra as indices of infants' patterns preferences. *Infant Behavior and Development, 10,* 49-59.

Kleiner, K., & Banks, M. S. (1987). Stimulus energy does not account for 2-month-olds' infants face preferences. *Journal of Experimental Psychology: Human Perception and Performance, 13,* 594-600.

Meltzoff, A. N., & Moore, M. K. (1977). Imitation of facial and manual gestures by human neonates. *Science, 198,* 75-78.

Meltzoff, A. N., & Moore, M. K. (1994). Imitation, memory, and the representation of persons. *Infant Behavior and Development, 17,* 83-99.

Schwarzer, G. (2000). Development of face processing: The effect of face inversion. *Child Development, 71,* 391-401.

Schwarzer, G. (2002). Processing of facial and non-facial visual stimuli in 2-5-year-old children. *Infant and Child Development, 11,* 253-269.

Schwarzer, G. & Korell, M. (2001). Gesichterwahrnehmung im Kleinkind- und Vorschul-alter. *Zeitschrift für Entwicklungspsychologie und Pädagogische Psychologie, 33,* 78-90.

Schwarzer, G., & Zauner, N. (2002). Face processing in 8-month-old infants: The role of specific facial features. Manuscript under revision.

Slater, A., Bremner, G., Johnson, S. P., Sherwood, P., Hayes, R., & Brown, E. (2000). Newborn infants' preference for attractive faces: The role of internal and external facial features. *Infancy, 1,* 265-274.

Slater, A., Quinn, P. C., Hayes, R., & Brown, E. (2000). The role of orientation in newborn infants' preference for attractive faces. *Developmental Science*, *3*, 181-185.

Tanaka, J. W., Kay, J. B., Grinnell, E., Stansfield, B., & Szechter, L. (1998). Face recognition in young children: When the whole is greater than the sum of its parts. *Visual Cognition*, *5*, 479-496.

Valenza, E., Simion, F., Macchi Cassia, V., & Umilta, C. (1996). Face preference at birth. *Journal of Experimental Psychology: Human Perception and Performance*, *27*, 892-903.

Ward, T. B. (1989). Analytical and holistic modes of processing in category learning. In B. E. Shepp & S. Ballesteros (Eds.), *Object perception: Structure and process* (pp. 387-419). Hillsdale, NJ: Erlbaum.

Yin, R. K. (1969). Looking at upside down faces. *Journal of Experimental Psychology*, *81*, 141-145.

Young, A. W., Hellawell, D., & Hay, D. C. (1987). Configural information in face perception. *Perception*, *16*, 747-759.

Younger, B. (1992). Developmental change in infant categorization: The perception of correlations among facial features. *Child Development*, *63*, 1526-1535.

Zauner, N. & Schwarzer, G. (2002). Gesichtsverarbeitung im ersten Lebensjahr. *Zeitschrift für Entwicklungspsychologie und Pädagogische Psychologie*. Manuscript under revision.

Address for Correspondence

Gudrun Schwarzer
Friedrich-Miescher-Laboratory of the
Max Planck Society
Spemannstr. 34
D-72076 Tübingen
Germany
E-mail: gudrun.schwarzer@tuebingen.mpg.de

Development of Face Processing in Early Adolescence

Helmut Leder

Gudrun Schwarzer

Steve Langton

5.1 Introduction

Whereas the previous chapter described the development of face processing during the first decade of life, in the present chapter we focus on the development of face recognition skills during early adolescence, that is, in children between 10 and 16 years of age. Implicit in most theories of face recognition is the hypothesis that face processing improves linearly with age, reaching a plateau of high performance in young adults, and remains more or less stable throughout life. The age range from 10 years onwards is of particular interest as there is some evidence that during this time face processing skills take a brief step backwards, casting some doubt on the linear increase hypothesis. In the first part of the chapter, we give a short overview on the development of face recognition in childhood and early adolescence and discuss some explanations for changes in face recognition performance in this age range. In the second part, we present two studies in which different explanations for changes in face recognition performance were tested.

5.1.1 Face Recognition in Childhood and Early Adolescence

Several studies have shown that there is a significant increase in face recognition performance in the 6 to 10 year old age group (Blaney & Winograd, 1978; Carey & Diamond, 1977; Carey, Diamond, & Woods 1980; Chung & Thomson, 1995; Flin, 1980; see Chapters 4, 9). There are two possible reasons for this improvement: 6-year-old children may have difficulty forming adequate representations of new faces that will serve to distinguish them from all the other faces they may have encountered. Children might also have more problems than adults matching the representation of a current face with a representation stored in memory. The evidence available points towards the problem of being one of encoding a new face when it is first presented, rather than in actually recognizing it when tested. For example, 6-year-olds are poor at deciding whether two simultaneously presented pictures are of the same person if the photographs differ in terms of their lighting, angle of viewpoint, facial expression or the clothing worn (e.g., Diamond & Carey, 1977; Flin, 1980). It was shown that these developmental changes in face processing were not due to a general increase in the ability to encode complex pattern, but instead reflect the acquisition of some kind of face-specific expertise (Diamond & Carey, 1990).

While most evidence suggests that there is a linear trend for the increase in face recognition skills up to the age of 10, the few studies carried out with older children suggest that this increase does not continue after about 11 to 13 years of age (Chung & Thomson, 1995; Diamond, Carey & Back, 1983; Goldstein, 1975; Soppe, 1986). Figure 1 shows the results from 3 studies with 6- to 16-year-olds indicating these differences in developmental course.

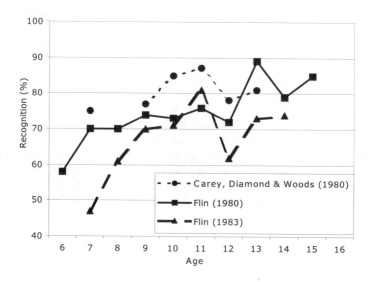

Figure 1. Samples of developmental courses from three studies.

As can be seen, the studies carried out by Carey, Diamond, and Woods (1980) and Flin (1983) actually reveal a dip in performance between the ages of 10 and 16 years, mainly around the age of 12 years. Flin (1980), however, observes a leveling-off of performance rather than a decline around the age of 12 years followed by an increase of performance in older children.

Concerning the dip, Carey (1992) remarked: "As children get older, we expect them to get better at just about anything. This is why the decline in performance at age 12 seems the aspect of the developmental function most in need of explanation" (p. 96). In the next section we discuss some explanations for the dip before we present our studies.

5.1.2 Explanations for the Developmental Dip

Broadly speaking, there have been two kinds of explanation put forward to account for the dip in face recognition performance in older children. The first suggests that the dip is the result of a change in encoding strategy which develops to cope with the increasing number of faces children encounter. This change is unrelated to the maturational status of the child; for example, a similar dip could be experienced by an adult when acquiring a new class of information. One piece of evidence in favor of this reason for the dip is the change of environment often experienced by children around the age of 12. At about this age, children in the U.K. and the United States move from small elementary schools to larger institutions. One possibility is that the number of new faces that the child has to encode during this period interferes with the encoding of new faces in an experimental situation. This interference would then lead to lower face recognition performance. Another possibility is that in order to cope with the increasing number of faces, children try to develop a new encoding strategy. Carey (1981) suggested that a typical shift in strategy might see the child attempting to use relatively superficial properties to distinguish faces, which would, of course, result in poorer performance. For evidence of a change in encoding style, Haas and Sporer (1993) refer to studies carried out explicitly to find out how children of different ages describe faces. They conclude that there is clear evidence that younger children tend to use rather feature-based descriptions while older children use more interpretative descriptions. Others (Carey, 1978; Flin, 1983) have suggested that the decline in face recognition performance may reflect changes in cognitive strategy from one with which the child is already proficient, to another potentially more effective strategy. In the transition period the child may stop using the old strategy in favor of the new one which will not have been fully mastered, resulting in a concomitant decline in performance.

In contrast, the second type of explanation suggests that the dip is the result of changes associated with genetically programmed maturational development. The most obvious change that children undergo between 12 and 14 years of age is puberty and there is some evidence that it is implicated in the developmental dip. Diamond, Carey, and Back (1983) report two studies in which girls undergoing pubertal change, regardless of their age, performed worse in a face recognition test than age matched controls who had passed – or who had yet to reach – puberty. Furthermore, since most of the girls tested by Diamond et al. (1983) were in the same school grade, it seems unlikely that the switch from a small to a larger school is the cause of the dip. Also, this result seems to rule out explanations based on reorganizing face knowledge or changing encoding strategies merely as a function of age, since the dip was related to pubertal change, regardless of the age at which the change occurred.

Two types of explanation have been put forward to explain the changes in face recognition skills due to puberty: first, hormonal changes at puberty might have a direct effect on the brain areas involved in face encoding; second, maturational changes during this period might cause children to attend to different aspects of faces – a kind of indirect effect of puberty on face encoding with no implication of any changes in the neural substrate for face processing. In support of the direct, biological explanation, Carey (1981) cites work by Leehey (1976) on hemispheric specialization. In adults the right hemisphere is particularly involved in the recognition of complex objects such as faces. Leehey's work revealed that until the age of 10, children show a *left* hemispheric activation in face processing, while after the age of 10 specialization of the right hemisphere evolves. Between the ages of 12 and 14 Leehey observed a decrease in the right hemisphere advantage for face processing which is consistent with the hypothesis of maturation at puberty influencing face encoding mechanisms in the brain directly. However, as Chung and Thomson (1995) pointed out in their review, this reduced right hemisphere advantage at puberty has not been found in other studies.

Both Diamond et al. (1983) and Soppe (1986) have suggested that maturational changes at puberty influence face processing via an indirect path. The idea is that as children mature their interests in people change. As a result, children might attend to different aspects of faces resulting in a period of inefficient encoding (Diamond et al., 1983). Similarly, Soppe (1986) suggested that physiognomic changes at puberty may cause adolescents to attend to aspects of others' faces that are not particularly useful for recognition. Other hypotheses were that the disruption to encoding might occur as faces gain a specific social meaning such as attractiveness for the pubertal child, or that children simply attend to different aspects of people other than their faces (Soppe, 1986). As yet, none of these hypotheses has received much support. Our own study, reported in the next section, was – in part – an attempt to rectify this situation. Thus, changes due to puberty might also affect the encoding of either same or different gender faces differentially and might be marked by a gradual shift in attention to peer or adult faces. Chung and Thomson (1995) point out that children's face recognition abilities may have been underestimated when only adult faces were used.

5.2 Social Age Effects in Face Recognition: Study 1

In our study we investigated face recognition skills in school children of four age groups, covering an age range of about 9 to 15 years. Gender and age of the stimuli were systematically varied and the data were analyzed in a design using the gender of the children as a quasi-experimental factor. First, we were attempting to find further evidence about the course of development in face recognition skills in this age range, and to see whether a dip which some have suggested would occur at approximately 12 years of age. Second, the design allowed us to explore some hypotheses concerning the dip. If, as suggested by Soppe (1986), the dip occurs because of the opposite-gender meaning attached to faces by the pubertal child, we might expect to find particularly large effects in the processing of opposite sex faces. Similarly, changes in puberty might be marked by a shift in attention to either peer or adult faces. Finally, because males reach puberty later, we might expect them to experience any developmental dip later than females.

One hundred and thirty-six pupils from two schools (see Acknowledgements) in Berlin took part in our study. We set the following thresholds for the age groups and tried to make the age groups as comparable as possible: in the first age group, children ranged from 9.9 years to 11.3 years of age and there were 16 females and 15 males; in the second group, the boundaries were 11.4 to 12.7 years with 16 females and 13 males; in group 3, the ages ranged from 12.8 to 14.1 years and there were 25 females and 18 males; finally in group 4, the children were aged between 14.2 and 15.6 years and there were 27 females and only 6 males.

The study took the form of a classical recognition test in which children were first exposed to grayscale photographs of 20 faces in the encoding phase, and later, in the test phase, to 40 faces consisting of the 20 faces from the encoding phase and 20 new faces. Half the faces used in the encoding phase were female, the other half were male faces. Moreover, half the faces of each gender were faces of adults and half were of children. The distractor faces in the test phase followed the same classification. Thus, each set of targets and distractors consisted of faces of 5 female children, 5 male children, 5 female adults, and 5 male adults.

Children were presented with the first 20 faces, one at a time in a randomized order, each for three seconds and were asked to "look at each face carefully and decide in your mind whether the face is younger or older than you." Pretests had revealed that this instruction was appropriate to ensure that children attended to the faces and that sufficient processing took place for them to be recognized in a later test. Faces were presented in the same order to all 4 age groups of children. After a short break, all participants took part in the test phase of the experiment. Children were presented with the 20 faces from the encoding phase and 20 distractor faces in a random order and, for each face, they were asked to indicate whether or not it had been encountered in the first block of faces. Again, the same order was used for each of the age groups. The participants used a response sheet and indicated by ticking small boxes whether a face was "old, familiar" or "new, previously unseen."

Results were analyzed in terms of hit rates (the proportion of faces in the test phase correctly identified as having appeared in the first phase of the experiment) as well as false-alarm rates (the proportion of distractor faces incorrectly identified as having appeared in the first phase). The two measures were separated to test Soppe's finding (1986) that either measure can be affected by age separately.

Hit rates: Figure 2 illustrates the performance of the four age groups of children in correctly recognizing faces of their own and of the opposite gender as having been encountered in the first phase of the experiment. All groups of children were able to cope with the experimental task, correctly recognizing over 70% of the faces they had encountered in the first phase of the experiment. In terms of differences in performance between the age groups, hit rates in the two youngest groups were similar, as were those in the two oldest groups of children. In addition, children in these two older groups generally out-performed their younger counterparts. The performance of male children in recognizing female faces was, however, at odds with this general pattern of results. Boys in the second age group performed much better with female faces than their counterparts in the younger and older groups.

An analysis of variance using gender of the children (GENDER) and their age (AGECLASS (1 to 4)) as between-subject variables and gender of the stimuli (GENDFACE) and age of the stimuli (AGEFACE (child or adult faces)) as within-subject factors was conducted on the hit rate scores. The analysis revealed no main effects, but an interaction between GENDER and AGEFACE, $F (1, 128) = 8.276$, $p < .01$, and a trend for a three-way interaction between GENDERFACE, GENDER and AGECLASS, $F (3, 128) = 2.318$, $p = .079$. The interaction between GENDER and AGEFACE showed that female participants generally recognized faces of children better than faces of older people, while there was no difference for male participants. This is a finding, which allows us to speculate that girls and young females have a higher face recognition ability for peers of either gender than for older individuals, which does not support the puberty - other sex attraction hypothesis. Nonetheless, the result indicates that gender of the stimuli in the recognition test might be critical, and that the effect of the stimuli is modified by the gender of the participants. This is clear indication that the stimuli are of social importance although it does (due to a lack of a distinctive influence of age) not directly refer to any of the hypotheses concerning the developmental dip.

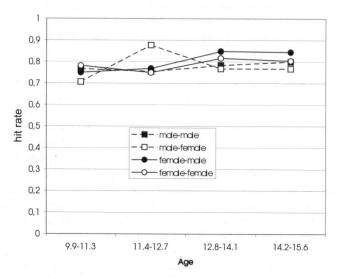

Figure 2. Hit rates in 9- to 15-year-olds (legend shows first: gender of participant and second: gender of the stimulus).

In sum, we found little evidence for a substantial improvement in performance between the ages of 9 and 15 years, nor was there any evidence for a dip in processing at approximately 12 years of age. Indeed, the most notable finding was actually a peak in the performance of male children with female faces at about this age.

False Alarm Rates: The proportion of distractor faces in the test phase which were incorrectly identified as having appeared in the first phase of the study is depicted in Figure 3. The number of false alarms was also submitted to an ANOVA. Once again age of participant (AGECLASS) and gender of participant (GENDER) were entered as between-subject factors, and gender of face (GENDERFACE) and age of face (AGEFACE) as within-subject factors. This analysis revealed a three-way interaction between age of participant (AGECLASS) and gender of participant (GENDER) and age of face (AGEFACE), $F (3, 128) = 3.598$, $p < .05$. This interaction is shown in Figure 3. Simple improvements in face processing performance between the age groups would be indicated by a general decrease in false alarm rates. This pattern can be seen in particular between age groups 1 (mean age = 10.6 years) and 2 (mean age = 12.1 years) in all but one condition (girls performance with peer's faces). In this condition the number of false alarms remained the same.

However, there are at least two conditions in which false alarm rates rise (i.e., performance deteriorates) in the older age groups. Interestingly these conditions are not the same for male and female pupils. While male pupils show an increase in false alarm rates when they see young faces (boys and girls), 13 to 15 year old female pupils show increased false alarm rates for faces of adults. We can only speculate here, but the data could be in accordance with an attentional explanation according to which mature girls and young women are more interested in adults and are therefore more likely not to identify these faces correctly, while male pupils, being less mature make mistakes with children's faces.

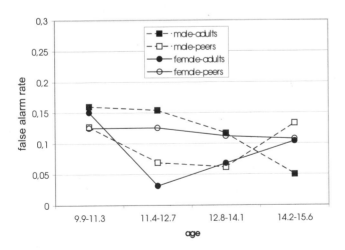

Figure 3. False alarm rates in 9- to 15-year-olds.

The results of our recognition study show no evidence of a developmental dip as some studies have suggested. However, when gender and age of the material to-be-recognized was varied systematically, we did find small but significant interactions with age (and gender) of the children.

5.3 Development of Configural Encoding

As already discussed, children's ability to encode faces certainly improves between the ages of 6 and 10 years. However, there has been some argument concerning exactly what it is that children get better at. Chung and Thomson (1995) concluded that children learn to encode more features quantitatively, as they get older. In other words, older children and adults just do more of what 6-year-olds can manage. On the other hand, Carey and Diamond (1994) maintain that expertise with faces reflects greater reliance on configural processing. In their view, older children and adults are doing something rather different with faces than their younger counterparts. Sensitivity to configural information is often measured indirectly by the size of the inversion effect (Leder & Bruce, 2000), which when adults were tested was usually bigger for configural as opposed to component information in faces. Carey and Diamond (1994) showed that the inversion effect for configural information increased between the ages of 6 and 10, supporting their claim that there is an increased reliance on configural information between these ages. Recently, Mondloch, Le Grand, and Maurer (2002) have shown that configural processing develops more slowly than the processing of component information until the age of 10. Changes in the mode of face processing during the first decade of life are also emphasized in Schwarzer's work (Schwarzer, 2000, see also Chapter 4). Here it could be shown that younger children use more featural information of faces whereas older children use more holistic information, comparing faces according to their overall similarity.

Thus, there is some evidence that 6-year-old children use both component and configural information but by 10 years of age they have become increasingly more reliant on using configural information to distinguish between faces. However, to our knowledge, there are no empirical studies which have investigated possible changes in sensitivity to configural processing over time after 10 years of age when the developmental dip has been observed. Therefore, in a second study we examined the sensitivity to differences in configural or component changes in upright and upside-down faces over the four age groups described in Study 1.

If the dip is related to changes in the sensitivity to configural information then we would expect this information to be processed poorly at about the age of 12, or to show differential effects of inversion. If the ability to encode and process faces has developed by the age of 10, then we would not expect effects of facial information or orientation to vary with the age of our participants.

5.3.1 Configural and Component Processing of Upright and Inverted Faces in 9- to 15-Year-Olds: Study 2

In Study 2 we examined the developmental course of sensitivity to configural or component information in 9- to 15-year-old children. The same participants as in Study 1 were tested. They were presented with pairs of faces and were asked to judge whether the faces were the same or different. Each pair consisted of pictures of the same individual and were either identical or could differ in one of two ways. Pairs might differ with respect to the configural arrangement of the features (e.g., the eyes might be moved further apart in one face compared to the other), or with respect to components (e.g., the eyes in one face might be different to those in the other face). Moreover, the pairs of faces were presented in either an upright or an inverted orientation, as sensitivity to configural processing is often found indirectly by the size of the inversion effect.

In this study, 18 different pairs of faces were used. Each pair of faces showed the same individual, and half of the pairs were of young adult males and the remaining half of young adult females. Of the 18 pairs, six consisted of identical pictures, six of the pairs showed the same individuals but a configural change was made to one of the pair, and in the remaining six pairs, a local featural change was made to one of the faces. Configural changes were made by manipulating the location of a facial feature, and component changes were made by exchanging either the eyes, nose, or mouth from one face for the same feature from another face. Each pair was presented twice: once in an upright orientation, and once in an inverted (i.e., upside down) orientation.

All faces used were artificial in that they were composed of components from different faces and rated for plausibility before being used in this test. The backgrounds in all of the pictures and the size of the images were standardized. There were, however, some variations in pose, hairstyle and expression, although we omitted features such as earrings etc. All faces were shown in grayscale and projected onto a screen using a video beamer.

The participants were instructed that they would see pairs of faces showing either the same face or two similar but different faces. For illustration purposes, the different types of pairs were presented and the differences explained to the participants. The response sheet included a number for each pair and two boxes for "same" and "different" responses. Pairs of faces were shown for seven seconds followed by a short interlude (of about 5 seconds) during which the children made their responses by marking the appropriate box on the response sheet. Pairs of faces were presented in the same randomized order to all the participants. The block took less than ten minutes.

As we were interested in testing whether sensitivity to component or configural features develops in early adolescence, we analyzed the correct responses in the different trials, in upright and inverted orientations. An ANOVA was carried out on the accuracy data with GENDER and AGECLASS as between-subject variables, and kind of INFORMATION (configural-component) and ORIENTATION (upright-inverted) as within-subject factors. This analysis revealed no effect of AGECLASS, but a significant effect of INFORMATION, $F(1, 128) = 76.02$, $p < .001$, with component information being recognized better, as well as a strong main effect of ORIENTATION, F (1, 128) = 134.72, p < .0001, and an interaction between ORIENTATION and INFORMATION, F (1, 128) = 6.842, p < .01.

Figure 4 shows the proportion of correct responses made by children in the different age groups to pairs of faces differing in configural or component information in both orientations. Differences in component information were recognized better than configural differences. Moreover, both sorts of information showed inversion effects but these were larger for configural information. The larger inversion effects when detecting configural differences are in accordance with the findings of other researchers and confirm that the test in general was sensitive to important features of face processing. Figure 4 also reveals that sensitivity to both local and configural information did not increase across age groups. Thus, it seems that sensitivity to configural and component information has developed by the age of 10 and does not interact with the age groups investigated here. However, from our test of configural sensitivity, which taps perceptual encoding, we cannot exclude the possibility that there are important changes in memory performance concerning different sorts of facial information.

5.4 Conclusion

Studies on the development of face recognition from the age of 10 to adulthood have revealed that there are often deviations from a purely linear increase. Several researchers have observed a dip around the age of 12 and have suggested that physiological or social changes in puberty might account for this reversal of development.

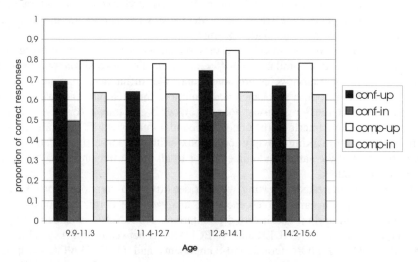

Figure 4. Effects of orientation (up-in) and age on the sensitivity to configural (conf) or componential (comp) changes.

Although our studies revealed some linear trends, we found no evidence of a dip. This is in accordance with another group of studies (reported in Chung & Thomson, 1995) in which no significant dip was found. Concerning the development of sensitivity to configural features, here again we found no evidence for a dip in the processing of faces. Neither was there a change in the relation between configural and component information with age, nor a change in sensitivity to orientation.

The results of the first study showed that the face recognition performance of 9- to 15-year-olds was influenced by an interaction between the gender of the participants and the age of the stimuli to be recognized. These results demonstrate that further research is needed to test the influence of gender, other effects at puberty and social changes on face recognition performance more explicitly. Recently, Bruce et al. (2000) have introduced a series of tests to examine the face processing skills of younger children. Developing similar standardized tests could be important for our understanding of face processing in young adolescents.

Acknowledgements

This research was supported by the DFG with a Grant to Leder (Le 1286). We want to thank Christine Glamann, Gesa Dohrmann, Eva Dräger and Sarah Späth for their help in conducting our studies. Moreover, we thank all teachers and pupils at the Sophie-Scholl-Oberschule as well as the Rothenburg Grundschule.

References

Blaney, R. L., & Winograd, E. (1978). Developmental differences in children's recognition memory for faces. *Developmental Psychology*, 14, 441-442.

Bruce, V., Campbell, R., McAuley, S., Doherty-Sneddon, G., Langton, S., Import, A., & Wright, R (2000). Testing face processing skills in children. *British Journal of Developmental Psychology*, *18*, 319-333.

Carey, S. (1978). A case study: Face recognition. In E. Walker (Ed.), *Explorations in the biology of language* (pp. 175-201). Montgomery, VT: Bradford Books.

Carey, S. (1981). The development of face recognition. In G. Davies, H. Ellis, & J. Shephard (Eds.), *Perceiving and remembering faces* (pp. 9-38). New York: Academic Press.

Carey, S. (1992). Becoming a face expert. *Philosophical Transactions of the Royal Society of London*, B335, 95-103.

Carey, S., & Diamond, R. (1977) Developmental changes in the representation of faces. *Journal of Experimental Child Psychology*, *23*, 1-22.

Carey, S., & Diamond, R. (1994). Are faces perceived as configurations more by adults than by children? *Visual Cognition, 1(2/3),* 253-274.

Carey, S., Diamond, R., & Woods, B. (1980). Development of face recognition – a maturational component? *Developmental Psychology, 16 (4)*, 257-269

Chung, M. S., & Thomson, D. M. (1995). Development of face recognition. *British Journal of Psychology*, *86*, 55-87.

Diamond, R., & Carey, S., (1977). Developmental changes in the representation of faces. *Journal of Experimental Child Psychology, 23*, 1-22.

Diamond, R., & Carey, S. (1990). On the acquisition of pattern encoding skills. *Cognitive development, 5*, 345-386.

Diamond, R., Carey, S., & Back, K. J. (1983). Genetic influences on the development of spatial skills during early adolescence. *Cognition, 13*, 167-185.

Flin, R. H. (1980). Age effects in children's memory for unfamiliar faces. *Developmental Psychology, 16*, 373-374.

Flin, R. H. (1983). The development of face recognition. Ph.D. thesis Aberdeen University (cited from Haas and Sporer, 1993).

Goldstein, A. G. (1975). Recognition of inverted photographs of faces by children and adults. *Journal of Genetic Psychology, 127*, 109-123.

Haas, S., & Sporer, S. L. (1993, April). Zur Entwicklung von Enkodierungsstrategien beim Wiedererkennen von Gesichtern [On the development of encoding strategies in the recognition of human faces]. (Abstract). (31. Tagung experimentell arbeitender Psychologen in Bamberg).

Leder, H., & Bruce, V. (2000). When inverted faces are recognised: The role of configural information in face recognition. *The Quarterly Journal of Experimental Psychology, A 53, (2)*, 515-536.

Leehey, S. C. (1976). Face recognition in children: Evidence for the development of right hemisphere specialisation. Unpublished PhD Thesis.MIT.

Mondloch, J. C., Le Grand, R., & Maurer, D. (2002). Configural face processing develops more slowly than featural face processing. *Perception, 31*, 553-566.

Schwarzer, G. (2000). Development of face processing: The effect of face inversion. *Child Development, 71*, 391-401.

Soppe, H. (1986). Children's recognition of unfamiliar faces: Developments and determinants. *International Journal of Behavioural Development, 9*, 219-233.

Address for Correspondence

Helmut Leder
Department of Psychology
Free University of Berlin
Habelschwerdter Allee 45
D-14195 Berlin
Germany
E-mail: leder@experimental-psychology.de

6

Expert Face Processing:
Specialization and Constraints

Adrian Schwaninger

Claus-Christian Carbon

Helmut Leder

6.1 Introduction

Face processing in adults is the product of innate mechanisms, and is also based on years of experience. There is no doubt that face processing is a human skill at which most adults are real experts. In the present chapter we review theories and hypotheses concerning adults' face processing skills, as well as what information and processes these are based on. Moreover, we discuss how the high specialization is attained at the cost of being susceptible to specific conditions.

Expertise, according to the American Heritage Dictionary is given when a person shows a high degree of skill in or knowledge of a certain subject. This definition implies that an expert is a high-grade *specialist*. Expertise does not have to be accessible in an explicit way, because an expert does not have to know all the facts of his expertise. The skill humans show in identifying faces is astonishing. According to Bahrick, Bahrick, and Wittlinger (1975) adults are able to recognize familiar faces with an accuracy of 90 per cent or more, even when some of those faces have not been seen for fifty years. Moreover, faces are a class of objects which encourage a special kind of categorization. According to the logic of Roger Brown's seminal paper "How shall a thing be called" (Brown, 1958), the level of the object name reflects the entry point of the recognition process. When asked to name pictures of faces spontaneously, humans produce the concrete names of the persons shown.

Classifying objects at this kind of subordinate level is typical of experts (Tanaka & Taylor, 1991). Expertise can not only be recognized by the frequency of subordinate-level classifications but also by the speed of word generation (Tanaka, 2001a): Adults identified faces as fast at the subordinate level (the name of the person) as at the basic level (e.g., "human"). This is clear evidence for a level of expertise.

To understand the development of face processing from childhood to adulthood better, we review the characteristics of information processing used by adults. First, we consider different types of pictorial information contained in faces. Then we review the holistic hypothesis as well as the schema hypothesis. This is followed by a discussion of important characteristics of adult face recognition, namely the sensitivity to configural information and the specialization in upright faces. Subsequently, the component configural hypothesis is discussed. Finally, we present a model for familiar and unfamiliar face recognition which allows the integration of several important aspects of a fully developed face processing system.

6.2 Information Contained in Faces

Faces are complex three-dimensional surfaces of the front side of the human head. Psychophysical studies using computer graphics have distinguished surface-based shape information from superficial properties such as color and texture (e.g., Hill, Schyns, & Akamatsu, 1997; Troje & Bülthoff, 1996).

Another commonly used distinction is based more on phenomenology. The term *component* information (or componential, piecemeal, featural information) has been used to refer to separable local elements, which are perceived as distinct parts of the whole such as the eyes, mouth, nose or chin (Carey & Diamond, 1977; Sergent, 1984). Components describe the basic primitives in faces, and the number of dimensions on which all components can differ provides the basis for all human faces being unique. A second type of information has been referred to as *configural* or *relational*. According to Bruce (1988), the term configural information refers to the "spatial interrelationship of facial features" (p. 38), i.e., features which come about from spatial arrangements, such as eye distances, nose-mouth distance. Distinctiveness correlates positively with the recognizability of faces, and Leder and Bruce (1998) revealed that component as well as configural information contribute to the distinctiveness of faces. Configural information was defined further by Diamond and Carey (1986). They used the term *first-order relational information* for the basic arrangement of the parts and *second-order relational information* to refer to specific metric relations between features.

The term *holistic* has been used to describe representations that store a face as an unparsed perceptual whole without specifying the parts explicitly. It has been operationalized in whole-to-part superiorities (see Section 6.3.1) and refers to properties and features when the face is processed as a Gestalt and not parsed into components (Farah, Tanaka, & Drain, 1995; Tanaka & Farah, 1993). A simple two-dimensional analogy for a holistic face representation would be a bitmap that only specifies the color values of points without providing any information about which points belong to the mouth or the eyes. Although the bitmap contains eyes and a mouth, it does not represent them explicitly[1].

These different types of information contained in faces are related to hypotheses about adult face processing which are discussed next.

6.3 Mechanisms of Face Processing in Adults

In order to explain the mechanisms used in adult face processing, several hypotheses have been proposed. According to the holistic hypothesis, adults process faces as unparsed perceptual wholes. The schema hypothesis assumes that the ability to process faces improves over many years and is attained at the expense of flexibility. This specialization could be related to adults' high sensitivity to configural information. Since faces are usually seen upright, it is not surprising that orientation is a critical variable for a face processing system that develops from years of experience. According to the component configural hypothesis, the processing of configural information is much more impaired by changes of orientation than the processing of component information. Why this might be the case is explained by the integrative model we propose after discussing each of these hypotheses in more detail.

6.3.1 Holistic Hypothesis

According to the holistic hypothesis, upright faces are stored as unparsed perceptual wholes in which individual parts (components) are not explicitly represented (Farah et al., 1995; Tanaka & Farah, 1993). Several empirical findings have been interpreted in favor of this view. For example, Tanaka and Farah (1993) reasoned that if face recognition relies on parsed representations, then a component (e.g., a nose) presented in isolation should be easy to recognize. In contrast, if faces are represented as unparsed perceptual wholes (i.e., holistically) then a part of a face presented in isolation should be much more difficult to recognize. In their experiments, participants were trained to recognize upright faces, each of which had a different pair of eyes, nose, and mouth. In the test phase, images of faces were presented in pairs. Each pair of faces differed only in the shape of one part of the face. In one test condition, two facial parts were presented in isolation. The subjects had to judge which of the two parts belonged to a face familiar from the training phase. In the whole face condition, the parts were embedded in the facial context. For example, one face contained the original nose and the other contained a different nose. The participants had to judge which of them was the face familiar to them from the training phase. Parts presented in isolation were more difficult to identify than whole faces. In contrast, when participants were trained to recognize inverted faces,

---

[1] Note that this definition is different from the concept of holistic processing, which is understood in terms of overall similarity relations (see Chapter 4).

scrambled faces, and houses no advantage of presenting the parts in their context was found. The authors interpreted this result in favor of the holistic hypothesis and proposed that face recognition relies mainly on holistic representations while the recognition of objects is based much more on part-based representations. Whereas encoding and matching parts are assumed to be relatively orientation-invariant (Biederman, 1987), holistic processing is thought to be very sensitive to orientation (see also Biederman & Kalocsai, 1997; Farah et al., 1995).

The results of a study conducted by Tanaka and Sengco (1997) provide further support for the holistic hypothesis, although their concept of holistic is slightly different. Instead of assuming that faces are processed as unparsed perceptual wholes, the authors reasoned that if *both component and configural information are combined* into a single holistic representation, changes in configural information should affect the recognition of facial parts (component information). This was precisely what was found in their first experiment: After training with upright faces, the subjects recognized components (eyes, nose and mouth) better in the unaltered facial context than in the context of a face in which the configural information had been changed by manipulating the distance between the eyes. If holistic processing is hampered by inversion and if face recognition relies much more on holistic representations than object recognition does, then a similar configural manipulation should have no effect on the recognition of parts of inverted faces or objects such as houses. This indeed was the case. The authors showed that configural manipulations did not affect the recognition of isolated parts when faces were presented upside-down nor did they do so when upright houses were used in the training and test conditions. (For faces, the alteration of configural information was accomplished by increasing the distance between the eyes, and for houses by manipulating the distance between the windows.) Thus, altering the configural information only affects the recognition of parts in the case of upright faces. This finding favors the view that in normal (upright) face processing the component and configural information is combined into a single holistic representation and that this holistic processing is disrupted by inversion. In Paragraph 6.3.3 we review further evidence for the importance of configural information in face processing.

Another line of evidence for this view is derived from a study carried out by Rhodes, Brake, and Atkinson (1993). These authors used (coarse) digitized versions of full-face photos in a recognition memory paradigm. Configural alterations, which were induced by altering the internal spacing of the eyes and mouth, were more difficult to recognize when faces were inverted. Interestingly, when the eyes or mouth were replaced with those of another face, effects of inversion were even more detrimental to recognition performance! Rhodes et al. (1993) concluded that either the component changes also affected the configural information or that the assumption that component processing is relatively unaffected by inversion is incorrect. The authors reasoned that if the replacement of components also resulted in a configural change and this caused the decrease in performance for inverted faces, then this effect of inversion should disappear when the components are presented alone. The results of their Experiment 2 favored this interpretation. In line with the results of Tanaka and Sengco (1997), the findings of Rhodes et al. (1993) are consistent with the view that in normal (upright) face processing component and configural information is combined into a single holistic face representation and that this holistic processing is impaired by inversion. Note that this concept of holistic processing differs slightly from the original definition of Tanaka and Farah (1993) and Farah et al. (1995). In the original view, holistic processing just means that parts are not represented explicitly. In contrast, holistic processing according to the results of Tanaka and Sengco (1997) and Rhodes et al. (1993) would imply that component and configural information are first encoded separately and then integrated into a holistic representation.

According to Farah et al. (1995) the holistic hypothesis also predicts that effects of inversion can be eliminated if participants are induced to represent faces in terms of their parts. Indeed, these authors found that inversion had the expected negative effect on the recognition of faces that were studied normally, while this impairment disappeared when faces were studied as parts (head outline, eyes, nose, and mouth presented simultaneously in different boxes). However, while the authors admit that it is possible to represent faces in terms of their components, they stress that performance is impaired by inversion because faces are usually represented holistically, i.e., parts are not represented explicitly.

An alternative definition of holistic processing of faces was tested by Macho and Leder (1998). Holistic processing could be achieved by an interactive feature processing in which the processing of one feature depends in general on the quality of another feature. In a similarity decision task using faces which systematically varied on two or three dimensions to target faces, they did not find evidence for this kind of interactive processing.

6.3.2 Schema Hypothesis

Goldstein and Chance (1980) have suggested another hypothesis. According to their view, the ability to process faces (i.e., the face schema) improves with exposure to them. These authors suggest that this improvement is attained at the expense of flexibility. Therefore, because faces are usually seen upright, it follows that recognition performance should improve with age, but performance with unusual stimuli such as inverted faces should decline through development. Their predictions have been supported by studies that investigated the development of face recognition (for reviews see Carey, 1992; Ellis, 1992; Johnston & Ellis, 1995). A study by Diamond and Carey (1986) provides another line of evidence in favor of the schema hypothesis. These authors used faces and dog profiles as stimuli. They found that the performance of novices was affected by inversion when tested with human faces but not when dog profiles had to be recognized. In contrast, there was an effect of inversion on dog experts' (dog show judges and breeders with an average of 31 years experience with dogs' appearance) recognition of dog profiles which was comparable to the observed effect of inversion on their recognition of human faces! This result was also found when bird and dog experts were shown bird and dog pictures, and their N170-ERP[2] component was compared: Approximately 164 ms after presentation, objects of expertise (dogs for dog experts; birds for bird experts) can be dissociated from objects from lower expertise categories (Tanaka, 2001b). Thus, based on the schema hypothesis, one would assume that this vast amount of object exposure has resulted in an expert-specific schema that is orientation sensitive because all the exemplars have usually been encountered in the upright position.

Goldstein and Chance did not elaborate on how a schema is used. Nevertheless, the linking element between the results discussed in the previous paragraph might be the processing of configural information in faces: The use of this special class of information could be an essential element of a holistic representation as proposed by Tanaka and Sengco (1997) and might also develop with age as well as the face schema.

6.3.3 Sensitivity to Configuration

Adult face recognition is characterized by a high sensitivity to configural information. For example, Haig (1984) showed for unfamiliar faces that configural alterations produced by changing the distance between facial features are sometimes detected at the visual acuity threshold level. Hosie, Ellis, and Haig (1988) found similar results using familiar faces. Kemp, McManus, and Pigott (1990) used two-tone images and found that the high sensitivity to configural information is reduced in negative or inverted images. While these studies were primarily concerned with the perceptual level, Bruce, Doyle, Dench, and Burton (1991) revealed a specialization for processing configural information at the level of memory processes. When tested, participants had to decide whether faces and houses were identical to the ones presented in a previous block or whether they had been altered configurally. Although the alterations were smaller for faces than for houses, participants were more sensitive in detecting them. Similar to the result of Kemp et al. (1990), this effect diminished when the stimuli were inverted. Leder and Bruce (2000) tested directly whether individual configural elements are represented in memory explicitly. They used a set of 8 faces, each of which differed only in a distinctive local configural feature such as a lowered mouth or a smaller eye-distance. In the test phase, they presented the whole face or the distinctive features in isolation or embedded into an empty head shape. Participants were surprisingly efficient at recognizing faces from the isolated configural elements. Moreover, all the experiments in Leder and Bruce (2000) revealed that the processing of configural information was particularly disrupted by inversion. The authors conclude that it is the reliance on configuration that is essential for adult's expertise at processing upright faces.

Thus, based on the review of recent studies, better processing of configural information seems to be applicable for adults rather than children. This is in accordance with findings that the limits of face processing are often accompanied by

---

[2] The N170 is a posterior negativity of the event-related potential (ERP) which reflects an early stage of face processing

a disruption of configural rather than other sorts of information. In the next paragraph we describe three effects which are known to be particularly related to adult face processing.

6.3.4 Testing for Limits: The Advantage of Being Upright

The remarkable ability of recognizing faces reliably is highly dependent on orientation. We have already shown how the holistic hypothesis and the use of configural information by adults suggest that orientation is a critical variable. Moreover, to process facial information reliably, a large amount of expertise is required (for a review see Carey, 1992; Chapter 4). Through years of practice, the face recognition system becomes more specialized but at the same time more limited to processing the upright orientation (schema hypothesis). In the following section we review three effects that illustrate this specialization in upright faces: the face inversion effect, the Thatcher illusion and the face composite illusion.

In order to investigate whether inversion particularly affects the recognition of faces, Yin (1969) used a forced-choice recognition paradigm with pictures of human faces, airplanes, houses, and stick figures of men in motion as stimuli. In one condition the stimuli were learnt and tested in the upright orientation. Upright faces were recognized better than all the other upright stimuli but were stronger affected by inversion. In another condition the stimuli were learnt in the upright orientation and then tested in the inverted orientation. Generally, when the stimuli had to be recognized in the upside-down position, error rates increased for all stimuli. The interesting finding was that this increase was disproportionately high for faces when compared with the other objects. Whilst faces were recognized best in the upright test condition, performance for inverted faces dropped below the recognition levels of the other object classes. This finding, namely that upside-down faces are disproportionately more difficult to recognize than other inverted objects, has been referred to as the *face inversion effect*. Subsequent replications of Yin's study have refined the initial methodology by comparing faces with stimuli that were equivalent in terms of familiarity, complexity, and psychosexual importance (e.g., Ellis, 1975; Goldstein & Chance, 1981; Scapinello & Yarmey, 1970). Valentine (1988) presented a comprehensive summary of studies investigating the face inversion effect. The review of recent results on holistic and configural processing suggests that the disruption of configural information explains most of the effects of the inversion of faces (Leder & Bruce, 2000).

Another impressive demonstration for the orientation-sensitive nature of face processing comes from a study carried out by Thompson (1980). In a photograph of Margaret Thatcher, he rotated the eyes and mouth within the facial context, which resulted in a grotesque facial expression (see Figure 1 for a demonstration). Interestingly, this strange expression is not perceived when the face is turned upside-down, but is immediately apparent when the face is turned upright. This effect has been referred to as the *Thatcher illusion*. It is clear that this manipulation of the orientation of components alters the form of the eyes and mouth to the point of grotesqueness.

Figure 1. Thatcher illusion. Both inverted pictures look more or less "normal". But when turned upright, the thatcherized version is seen to be highly grotesque. Try it!

Inverting the eyes within the facial context clearly changes the spatial relationship of the parts. Indeed, this alteration has been considered by some authors to produce a change in the configural information (e.g., Bartlett & Searcy, 1993; Diamond & Carey, 1986; Stevenage, 1995).

Young, Hellawell, and Hay (1987) discovered another interesting effect (see Figure 2 for an illustration). They created composite faces by combining the top and bottom half of different faces. If the two halves were aligned and presented upright, a new face resembling each of the two originals seemed to emerge. This made it very difficult to identify the persons from either half. If the top and bottom halves were misaligned horizontally, then the two halves did not fuse spontaneously to create a new face, and the constituent halves remained identifiable. However, when these stimuli were inverted, the constituent halves of the aligned and misaligned displays were equally identifiable. Furthermore, the subjects were significantly faster at naming the constituent halves in inverted composites than in upright composites.

Figure 2. Aligned and misaligned halves of different identities (here two of the authors). When upright (as above), a new identity seems to emerge from the aligned composites (left), which makes it more difficult to extract the original identities. This does not occur for the misaligned composite face (right). When viewed upside-down, the original identities can be extracted easily from both pictures.

Young et al. (1987) have argued that it is the new configuration in the composite face, which makes the identification of the parts difficult. Thus again we have evidence that an effect specific for upright faces might be due to the use of configural information in upright faces and the disruption of this in upside-down faces.

Concerning the developmental course, Cashon and Cohen (2001) showed that 7-month-old infants process composites from outer and inner features as one face. This may be taken as evidence for a kind of configural processing, which is in accordance with Tanaka, Kay, Grinnell, Stansfield, and Szechter (1998) who found that 6-year-olds showed the same whole-to-part superiority effects as adults. Carey and Diamond (1994) also found that adult-like composite effects emerge at the age of 6 while configural processing (indicated by inversion effects) develops continually until adulthood. Recently, Mondloch, Le Grand, and Maurer (2002) showed that configural processing develops later than featural or component processing and that it may still develop after the age of ten (see also Chapters 4 and 5).

6.3.5 Component Configural Hypothesis

While numerous studies have been presented which stress the importance of configural processing, it is not yet clear how different features are combined to form a representation of faces in memory. In the present paragraph we discuss a hypothesis in which two modes of processing are assumed: the component configural hypothesis. According to this hypothesis, component and configural information is processed separately, and configural processing is much more affected by changes of orientation than the processing of components. There is a large amount of evidence in favor of this view. The first demonstration of a differential effect of inversion on the processing of component and configural information was provided by Sergent (1984). She used pairs of faces where either the eyes or facial contour (change of component information) or the internal spacing of components (change of configural information) were mismatched. A multidimensional scaling technique for the analysis of dissimilarity judgments, and regression analyses on reaction times revealed that configural and component information were used for upright faces. In contrast, there was no evidence that subjects made use of configural information when faces were inverted. It should be noted, however, that Sergent (1984) used schematic faces which could make it difficult to generalize this result to the processing of real faces. However, similar results were found by Searcy and Bartlett (1996), who used color photographs of faces in which configural changes had been induced by moving the eyes and mouth up or down, and manipulation of the component information had been achieved by changing the color of the pupils and teeth or by shortening and elongating the teeth. In line with Sergent's (1984) results, a grotesqueness-rating task and a simultaneous paired-comparison task provided further evidence for the view that inversion is particularly disruptive to the processing of configural information. Leder and Bruce (1998) manipulated the distinctiveness of either components or configural features directly and showed how both make upright faces easier to recognize. When faces were presented upside-down, the effects of distinctiveness based on configural features vanished in nearly all conditions.

Another demonstration of the differential effects of orientation on the processing of component and configural information was provided by Schwaninger and Mast (1999). They used a sequential same-different matching task and found that the detection of component changes (eyes and mouth replaced) was relatively invariant to planar rotations. In contrast, rotation had a detrimental effect upon the detection of configural changes that were induced by increasing the distance between the eyes and the eyes and mouth (Figure 3). Interestingly, the effect of rotation on configural processing was nonlinear; most errors were found at intermediate angles of rotation between upright and inverted orientations, i.e., at 90°–120°. Similarly, Murray, Yong, and Rhodes (2000) found a discontinuity in the function relating bizarreness to a rotation of between 90° and 120° which was found for Thatcher faces and faces in which configural changes were induced by changing the relative position of the eyes and mouth. The bizarreness ratings of unaltered or component-distorted faces (teeth blackened and eyes whitened) showed only a linear trend. Leder and Bruce (2000, Experiment 5) compared directly whether configurations are also accessible when, at the same time, components vary from face to face: the isolated configurations, though composed of components which they shared with other faces, were recognized and showed inversion effects. To show directly that configural information is processed differentially in upright as compared to inverted faces, Leder, Candrian, Huber, and Bruce (2001) used a sequential comparison task. Participants saw two faces sequentially which differed in interocular eye-distance only. The task was to decide for each pair of faces which face had the larger interocular eye-distance. The judgments were more accurate when the faces were presented upright, and the decrement in accuracy in the inverted condition was independent of the size of the surrounding context (e.g., whether the nose or the mouth and nose were added).

One possible caveat of the studies that investigated the processing of component and configural information by replacing or altering facial features is that this type of manipulation often changes the holistic aspects of the face and is difficult to carry out selectively.

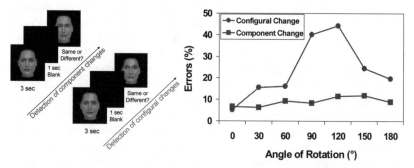

Figure 3. Study by Schwaninger and Mast (1999). Left: The detection of component and configural changes was tested using a sequential same-different matching task in separate experiments. Right: Whereas the identification of component changes was almost unaffected by rotation, the detection of configural changes was strongly impaired.

For example, replacing the nose (component change) can change the distance between the contours of the nose and the mouth and thus alter the configural information (Leder & Bruce, 1998; 2000). The same applies to configural changes when they are carried out by altering the relative position of the components. For example, moving the eyes apart (configural change) can lead to an increase in size of the bridge of the nose, i.e., a component change (see Leder et al., 2001).

Problems like these can be avoided by using scrambling and blurring procedures to reduce configural and component information separately (e.g., Collishaw & Hole, 2000; Davidoff & Donnelly, 1990; Sergent, 1985). Recently, Schwaninger, Lobmaier, and Collishaw (2002) used scrambling and blurring techniques in an old-new recognition paradigm. Their experiments extend previous research by ensuring that scrambling and blurring effectively eliminate configural and component information separately. Furthermore, in contrast to previous studies, Schwaninger et al. (2002) used the same faces in separate experiments on unfamiliar and familiar face recognition to avoid potential confounds with familiarity (Figure 4).

In Experiment 1, unfamiliar face recognition was studied. In the first condition it was shown that previously learnt intact faces could be recognized even when they were scrambled into constituent parts. This result challenges the assumption of purely holistic processing according to Farah et al. (1995) and suggests that facial features or components are encoded and stored explicitly. In a second condition, the blur level was determined that made the scrambled versions impossible to recognize. This blur level was then applied to whole faces in order to create configural versions that by definition did not contain local featural information. These configural versions of previously learnt intact faces could be recognized reliably. This result suggests that separate representations exist for component and configural information. Familiar face recognition was investigated in Experiment 2 by running the same conditions with participants who knew the target faces (all distractor faces were unfamiliar to the participants).

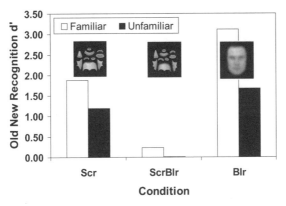

Figure 4. Recognition performance in unfamiliar and familiar face recognition across three different conditions at test. Scr: scrambled, ScrBlr: scrambled and blurred, Blr: blurred. (Adapted from Schwaninger, Lobmaier, & Collishaw, 2002)

Component and configural recognition was better when the faces were familiar, but there was no qualitative shift in processing strategy since there was no interaction between familiarity and condition (Figure 4).

In sum, there is converging evidence in favor of the view that separate representations for component and configural information exist which are relevant for the recognition of familiar and unfamiliar faces. Whereas component information is not very orientation-sensitive, configural information is difficult to recover when faces are rotated.

6.4 An Integrative View of Face Recognition

Everyday object recognition is often a matter of discriminating between quite heterogeneous object *classes* that differ with regard to their global shape, parts and other distinctive features such as color or texture. In contrast, face recognition relies on the discrimination of *exemplars* of a very homogenous category. All faces share the same basic parts in the same basic arrangement. In each face the eyes are above the nose which is located above the mouth. Therefore, reliable face recognition relies on the detection of subtle featural and configural differences, which needs years of experience. Since faces are usually seen upright, this learning must become more and more restricted to the upright orientation. A strong dependency on orientation is the consequence for objects that are usually perceived in one specific orientation. Since effects of rotation and inversion are much more detrimental for faces than for basic level object recognition, a certain type of information must be more relevant for faces. According to certain authors, expert face recognition is characterized by holistic processing (e.g., Biederman & Kalocsai, 1997; Farah et al., 1995; Tanaka & Farah, 1993). Farah et al. (1995) answer the question "Why is face recognition so orientation sensitive?" in the following way: "Face perception is holistic and the perception of holistically represented complex patterns is orientation sensitive." (p. 633). According to Rock (1973, 1974, 1988), rotated faces overtax an orientation normalization mechanism, which makes it impossible to match them against stored upright memory representations. Rotated faces can only be processed by their components, and configural information is hard to recover. This would explain why effects of rotation are much smaller for component as opposed to configural changes (Leder & Bruce, 1998, 2000; Schwaninger & Mast, 1999). At the same time, these results challenge a purely holistic view of face processing which assumes that explicit representations of facial parts do not exist. The recent results of Schwaninger et al. (2002) offer further evidence against such a purely holistic view. They revealed that facial components and configural information are encoded and stored explicitly, both in unfamiliar and familiar face recognition, when faces are upright.

In order to integrate the different hypotheses outlined in this chapter, we propose the model depicted in Figure 5. All pictorial aspects of a face are contained in the pictorial metric input representation which is presumably correlated with activation in primary visual areas. Based on years of expertise, neural networks are trained to extract specific information in order to activate component and configural representations in the ventral visual stream. The output of these representations converges towards the same identification units. These units are holistic in the sense that they integrate component and configural information. Note that this concept of holistic differs from the original definition of Tanaka and Farah (1993) and Farah et al. (1995). In their view, holistic means that parts are not represented explicitly. In contrast, according to our model, holistic processing implies that component and configural information are encoded separately first and then integrated into a holistic representation. Our concept of holistic is fully compatible with the results from Schwaninger et al. (2002) and Leder et al. (2001) who showed that featural and configural information is encoded explicitly. Moreover, our integrative definition of holistic is consistent with the results of Tanaka and Sengco (1997) and Rhodes et al. (1993) which imply that in normal (upright) face processing, component and configural information is combined into a single holistic face representation. Finally, our concept of holistic can be related to holistic processing in terms of overall similarity relations (see Chapter 4). A holistic similarity decision would be based on a linear or nonlinear integration of component and configural information, a prerequisite of a developed face processing system. An analytical similarity decision would mean that only component information is used to judge the similarity of faces.

Adult face recognition is characterized by the processing of configural information and by the fact that faces are quite hard to recognize when they are rotated substantially from the upright position. In the model this can be explained in the following way: When faces are rotated, the pictorial information in the input representation is changed remarkably. As a consequence, the component and configural representations which have been learnt based on exposure to upright faces, cannot be activated well enough to allow reliable recognition.

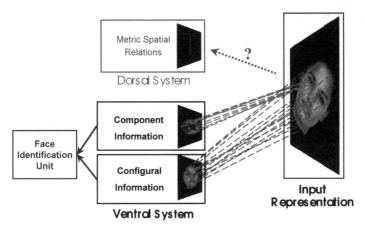

Figure 5. Integrative model of face processing. Facial information is encoded in a metric input representation that contains all the features we perceive in faces. Information of local features and relations between them is extracted in order to activate component and configural representations in the ventral stream. The outputs of these representations converge towards the same face identification units. Whether dorsal processing is relevant for processing metric spatial relations in faces such as the eye-mouth or the inter-eye distance remains to be investigated.

Rotated faces overtax orientation normalization mechanisms so that they have to be processed by their components (Rock, 1973, 1974, 1988). As pointed out by Valentine and Bruce (1988), this implies that information about the spatial relationship of components (configural information) is hard to recover. Consequently, the processing of configural information is much more affected by rotation or inversion than the processing of component information. Since face recognition relies heavily on processing configurations, the inversion effect is in disproportion to that of other objects (Yin, 1969). We believe that this is the deeper answer to the question "Why is face recognition so orientation sensitive?"

Our model also offers an explanation for the Thatcher illusion and the composite face illusion. Thatcherizing a face, i.e., inverting the eyes and mouth within an upright face, results in a strange activation pattern of component and configural representations. Consequently, the face looks very bizarre. When a thatcherized face is inverted, the activation of configural representations is strongly impaired due to the limitation in capacity of an orientation normalization mechanism. Consequently, the strange activation pattern of configural representations is reduced and the bizarre perception vanishes. Moreover, in an inverted Thatcher face the components themselves are in the correct orientation which results in a relatively normal activation of component representations. Consequently, inverted Thatcher faces appear relatively normal (Rock, 1988). Finally, the composite face illusion can be explained by similar reasoning. Aligned upright face composites contain new configural information resulting in a new perceived identity. Inverting the aligned composites reduces the availability of configural information and it is easier to access the two different face identification units based on the component information alone.

In short, the model we propose allows the integration of the component configural hypothesis and holistic aspects of face processing. It explains striking perceptual effects such as the Thatcher illusion and the composite face illusion. Most importantly, it provides an integrative basis for understanding special characteristics of adult face recognition such as the specialization in upright faces and the sensitivity to configural information.

Acknowledgments

The present paper was partially supported by a grant to Leder from the Deutsche Forschungsgemeinschaft (DFG Le-1286) and by a grant to Schwaninger from the European Commission (CogVis, IST-2000-29375).

References

Bahrick, H. P., Bahrick, P. O., & Wittlinger, R. P. (1975). Fifty years of memory for names and faces: A cross-sectional approach. *Journal of Experimental Psychology: General, 104*, 54-75.

Bartlett, J. C., & Searcy, J. (1993). Inversion and configuration of faces. *Cognitive Psychology, 25*(3), 281-316.

Biederman, I. (1987). Recognition-by-components: a theory of human image understanding. *Psychological Review, 94*(2), 115-147.

Biederman, I., & Kalocsai, P. (1997). Neurocomputational bases of object and face recognition. *Philosophical Transactions of the Royal Society of London, B, 352*, 1203-1219.

Brown, R. (1958). How shall a thing be called? *Psychological Review, 65*, 14-21.

Bruce, V. (1988). *Recognising faces*. Hillsdale, NJ: Lawrence Erlbaum Associates.

Bruce, V., Doyle, T., Dench, N., & Burton, M. (1991). Remembering facial configurations. *Cognition, 38*, 109-144.

Carey, S. (1992). Becoming a face expert. *Philosophical Transactions of the Royal Society of London, 335*, 95-103.

Carey, S., & Diamond, R. (1977). From piecemeal to configurational representation of faces. *Science, 195*, 312-314.

Carey, S., & Diamond, R. (1994). Are faces perceived as configurations more by adults than by children? *Visual Cognition, 1*, 253-274.

Cashon, C., & Cohen, L. (2001). Do 7-month-old infants independent features of facial configurations? *Infant and child development, 10*, 83-92.

Collishaw, S. M., & Hole, G. J. (2000). Featural and configurational processes in the recognition of faces of different familiarity. *Perception, 29*, 893-910.

Davidoff, J., & Donnelly, N. (1990). Object superiority: A comparison of complete and part probes, *Acta Psychologica, 73*, 225–243.

Diamond, R., & Carey, S. (1986). Why faces are and are not special: An effect of expertise. *Journal of Experimental Psychology: General, 115*, 107-117.

Ellis, A. W. (1992). Cognitive mechanisms of face processing. In V. Bruce, A. Cowey, A. W. Ellis, & D. P. Perrett (Eds.), *Processing the facial image* (pp. 113-119). New York: Clarendon Press.

Ellis, H. (1975). Recognizing faces. *British Journal of Psychology, 66*, 409-426.

Farah, M. J., Tanaka, J. W., & Drain, H. M. (1995). What causes the face inversion effect? *Journal of Experimental Psychology: Human Perception and Performance, 21*, 628-634.

Goldstein, A. G., & Chance, J. E. (1980). Memory for faces and schema theory. *Journal of Psychology, 105*, 47-59.

Goldstein, A. G., & Chance, J. E. (1981). Laboratory studies of face recognition. In G. M. Davies, H. D. Ellis, & J. W. Sheperd (Eds.), *Perceiving and remembering faces*. London: Academic Press.

Haig, N. D. (1984). The effect of feature displacement on face recognition. *Perception, 13*(5), 505-12.

Hill, H., Schyns, P. G., & Akamatsu, S. (1997). Information and viewpoint dependence in face recognition. *Cognition, 62*, 201-222.

Hosie, J. A., Ellis, H. D., & Haig, N. D. (1988). The effect of feature displacement on the perception of well-known faces. *Perception, 17*, 461-474.

Johnston, R.A., & Ellis, H.D. (1995). The development of face recognition. In T. Valentine (Ed.), *Cognitive and computational aspects of face recognition, explorations in face space* (pp. 1-23). London, New York: Routledge.

Kemp, R., McManus, C., & Pigott, T. (1990). Sensitivity to the displacement of facial features in negative and inverted images. *Perception, 19*, 531-543.

Leder, H., & Bruce, V. (1998). Local and relational aspects of face distinctiveness. *Quarterly Journal of Experimental Psychology, 51A*, 449-473.

Leder, H., & Bruce, V. (2000). When inverted faces are recognized: The role of configural information in face recognition. *Quarterly Journal of Experimental Psychology, 53A*, 513-536.

Leder, H., Candrian, G., Huber, O., & Bruce, V. (2001). Configural features in the context of upright and inverted faces. *Perception, 30*, 73-83.

Macho S., & Leder H. (1998). Your eyes only? A test of interactive influence in the processing of facial features. *Journal of Experimental Psychology: Human Perception and Performance, 24(5)*, 1486-1500.

Mondloch, C. J., Le Grand, R., & Maurer, D. (2002). Configural processing develops more slowly than feature face processing. *Perception, 31*, 553-566.

Murray, J. E., Yong, E., & Rhodes, G. (2000). Revisiting the perception of upside-down faces. *Psychological Science, 11*, 498-502.

Rhodes, G., Brake, S., & Atkinson, A.P. (1993). What's lost in inverted faces? *Cognition, 47*, 25-57.

Rock, I. (1973). *Orientation and form.* New York: Academic Press.

Rock, I. (1974). The perception of disoriented figures. *Scientific American, 230*, 78-85.

Rock, I. (1988). On Thompson's inverted-face phenomenon (Research Note). *Perception, 17*, 815-817.

Scapinello, F. F., & Yarmey, A. D. (1970). The role of familiarity and orientation in immediate and delayed recognition of pictorial stimuli. *Psychonomic Science, 21*, 329-331.

Schwaninger, A., & Mast, F. (1999). Why is face recognition so orientation-sensitive? Psychophysical evidence for an integrative model. *Perception (Suppl.), 28*, 116.

Schwaninger, A., Lobmaier, J., & Collishaw, S. M. (2002). Role of featural and configural information in familiar and unfamiliar face recognition. *Lecture Notes in Computer Science, 2525*, 643-650.

Searcy, J. H., & Bartlett, J. C. (1996). Inversion and processing of component and spatial-relational information of faces. *Journal of Experimental Psychology: Human Perception and Performance, 22*, 904-915.

Sergent, J. (1984). An investigation into component and configurational processes underlying face recognition. *British Journal of Psychology , 75*, 221-242.

Sergent, J. (1985). Influence of task and input factors on hemispheric involvement in face processing. *Journal of Experimental Psychology: Human Perception and Performance, 11(6)*, 846-61.

Stevenage, S. V. (1995). Expertise and the caricature advantage. In T. Valentine (Ed.), *Cognitive and computational aspects of face recognition, explorations in face space* (pp. 24-46). London: Routledge.

Tanaka, J. W. (2001a). The entry point of face recognition: Evidence for face expertise. *Journal of Experimental Psychology: General, 130*, 534-543.

Tanaka, J. W. (2001b). A neural basis for expert object recognition. *Psychological Science, 12*, 43-47.

Tanaka, J. W., & Farah, M. (1993). Parts and wholes in face recognition. *Quarterly Journal of Experimental Psychology, 46*, 225-245.

Tanaka, J. W., & Sengco, J. A. (1997). Features and their configuration in face recognition. *Memory and Cognition, 25*, 583-592.

Tanaka, J. W., & Taylor, M. (1991). Object categories and expertise: Is the basic level in the eye of the beholder? *Cognitive Psychology, 23*, 457-482.

Tanaka, J. W., Kay, J. B., Grinnell, E., Stansfield, B., & Szechter, L. (1998). Face recognition in young children: When the whole is greater than the sum of its parts. *Visual Cognition, 5*, 479-496.

Thompson, P. (1980). Margaret Thatcher – A new illusion. *Perception, 9*, 483-484.

Troje, N. F., & Bülthoff, H. H. (1996). Face recognition under varying poses: The role of texture and shape. *Vision Research, 36(12),* 1761-1771.

Valentine, T. (1988). Upside-down faces: a review of the effect of inversion upon face recognition. *British Journal of Psychology, 79,* 471-491.

Valentine, T., & Bruce, V. (1988). Mental rotation of faces. *Memory and Cognition, 16,* 556-566.

Yin, R. K. (1969). Looking at upside-down faces. *Journal of Experimental Psychology, 81,* 141-145.

Young, A. W., Hellawell, D. J., & Hay, D. C. (1987). Configural information in face perception. *Perception, 16,* 747-759.

Address for Correspondence

Adrian Schwaninger
Max Planck Institute for Biological Cybernetics
Spemannstraße 38
D-72076 Tübingen
Germany
E-mail: adrian.schwaninger@tuebingen.mpg.de

Part III:
Applied Research on Face Processing in the Course of Development

A Framework for the Study and Treatment of Face Processing Deficits in Autism

James W. Tanaka

Samantha Lincoln

Logan Hegg

7.1 Introduction

From the moment of birth, newborns come into the world programmed with an innate preference for faces (Morton & Johnson, 1991). At the neurological level, distinct brain areas separately code information about the identity (Kanwisher, McDermott, & Chun, 1997) and emotional expression (Whalen et al., 1998) of a face. Beyond the simple recognition of its identity and emotion, what other purpose does the human face serve that would require such specialized neural machinery? In this chapter, we argue that faces provide an important channel for communicating personal information, such as one's thoughts and feelings, to other people. We claim that this ability to understand and respond to facial cues is a fundamental skill that individuals must acquire in order to become full participants in a larger social environment. Given the importance of face processing abilities, it is therefore not surprising that this type of social expertise is achieved by most people at a relatively early age of development.

Although it is true that most people are social experts in their ability to decode facial information, an accumulating body of evidence indicates that individuals with autism and Asperger's Syndrome lack many of the rudimentary skills necessary for successful face communication. Autism is clinically diagnosed as impaired socialization and communicative abilities in the presence of restricted patterns of behavior and interests (DSM-IV; American Psychiatric Association, 1994). Children with Autism

Spectrum Disorder (ASD) frequently fail to respond differentially to faces over non-face objects, are impaired in their ability to recognize facial identity and expression, and are unable to interpret the social meaning of facial cues.

In this chapter, we propose a hierarchical model that describes three major domains of information processing involved in the perception, recognition, and communication of facial cues. We discuss the behavioral and neurological evidence to support the validity of these domains in normal populations and how they are adversely affected by autism and Asperger's syndrome. In the third section of the chapter, we describe a computer-based instructional program *Let's Face It!* which develops a child's face processing skills. In the *Let's Face It!* program, specific face processing skills (e.g., recognition of facial expression) are enhanced and strengthened in a game-like format. We discuss ways in which the program can be used as an intervention tool for teaching face recognition and communication skills to ASD children.

7.2 A Hierarchical Model for Face Processing

According to the Hierarchical Face Processing Model (shown in Figure 1), everyday face processing requires several stages of analysis or processing domains. Each processing domain in the model has its own functional characteristics, goals, and neural substrates. According to this model, face processing begins with the Domain I ability to abstract face stimuli from other stimuli in the visual environment. Domain II examines the separable processes required for the recognition of facial identity and emotion. Domain III describes the use of facial information as it is applied to the communication of thoughts and feelings within a social context. The face processing model is structured so that each domain builds on the processes of the previous domains. In the following chapter, we will describe the general characteristics of the individual processing domains and discuss how autism affects the operation and performance of these domain abilities.

7.2.1 DOMAIN I: Selective Processing of Faces

The first domain of face processing concerns a level so basic and fundamental that it is easily overlooked – simply attending to faces. When viewing a photograph or a painting, our eyes usually travel first and most frequently to the faces in the picture. Few people can recall from memory, for example, the landscape in the background behind the Mona Lisa or the cut of van Gogh's suit. Thus, from a very early age, humans regard faces as "special" or distinct from other kinds of objects in the environment. This early preference for faces can be demonstrated in experiments where 3- and 6-month-old infants look longer at face-like stimuli than non-face like stimuli (Fantz, 1963). These results, however, do not necessarily imply that face preference is biologically hardwired as a vast amount of learning takes place in the first few months of life. Stronger evidence for the biological position was provided by Morton and Johnson's study (1991) where neonates, a mere 30 minutes old, preferentially oriented to face stimuli over non-face stimuli. Given that 30 minutes is not enough time for significant learning to occur, these findings suggest that humans are born with an innate preference to attend to faces.

While faces command the attention of normally developing infants, they do not seem "special" to children with autism. A retrospective study (Osterling & Dawson, 1994) reviewed videotapes depicting the first birthday parties of children with ASD and control children. The experimenters blindly coded the child's interactions for social, affective, and communicative behaviors. The videotapes showed that children who were subsequently diagnosed with autism spent significantly less time looking at people's faces during the party than the control children. In fact, some authors report that infants who were later diagnosed with ASD exhibit "face avoidance" where they preferentially attend to non-face objects over faces (Swettenham et al., 1998). Thus, it appears that by the first year of life, children with autism and Asperger's syndrome are less engaged by faces than typically developing children.

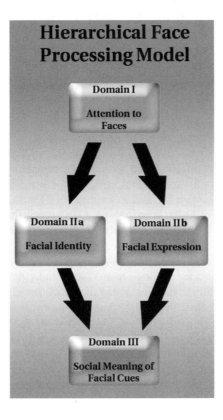

Figure 1. Diagram of Hierarchical Face Processing Model depicting the three domains of processing involving the perception of faces (Domain I), the recognition of facial identity (Domain IIa) and expression (Domain IIb), and the understanding of facial cues in a social setting (Domain III).

With regard to memory for face and non-face objects, individuals with autism do not differ from IQ-matched control participants in their ability to remember animate (e.g., horses, motorcycles) or inanimate objects (e.g., buildings). ASD individuals do, however, perform below control participants in their ability to remember faces (Blair, Frith, Smith, Abell, & Cipolotti, 2002). Thus, ASD children are not generally impaired in their memory for objects, but are specifically impaired in their memory for faces. In summary, whereas most children preferentially orient and recall faces over other types of objects, faces fail to achieve a privileged status in the perceptions or memories of children with autism.

The neurological evidence concerning face perception enriches our interpretation of the behavioral research and suggests a possible location for the processes of Domain I. In normal populations, brain imaging techniques have revealed the fusiform gyrus, a structure in the superior temporal area of the brain, to be significantly more activated by face stimuli relative to stimuli of other common objects (Kanwisher et al., 1997). Recently, Schultz and colleagues (Schultz et al., 2000) reported that when a group of adolescents with Asperger's Syndrome viewed pictures of faces, there was a *reduction* in fusiform gyrus activity relative to other non-face objects. Interestingly, when the Asperger's group viewed face stimuli, the inferior temporal gyrus was more activated than the fusiform area. In normal populations, this brain region is associated with object recognition, suggesting that faces may be perceived by people with autism not as entities of social agency, but as static non-social objects.

7.2.2 DOMAIN IIa: Recognition of Facial Identity

In Domain I, faces are differentiated from other competing objects in the visual environment. In Domain II, specific information about the face stimulus is derived regarding its identity (Domain IIa) and its expression (Domain IIb).

Within a few hours of birth, infants show a preference for their mother's face as compared to the face of strangers (Bushnell, Sai, & Mullin, 1989; Pascalis, de Schonen, Morton, Deruelle, & Fabre-Grenet, 1995). Thus, at a very early point in development, neonates can make within-category discriminations with respect to facial identity (i.e., this face belongs to a unique individual). By the age of six, normally developing children have extended their abilities to the recognition of faces which were unfamiliar before the testing situation and by the age of twelve, their face processing skills approach adult levels (Carey, Diamond, & Woods, 1980). Although the literature is not always consistent (Adolphs, Sears, & Piven, 2001), the prevailing view is that children with autism and Asperger's syndrome suffer specific deficits in their ability to distinguish facial identity (Boucher & Lewis, 1992; Hauck, Fein, & Maltby, 1999). In a carefully controlled study, Klin and colleagues (1999) tested the face recognition, Gestalt closure and spatial memory abilities of 102 young children with autism, pervasive developmental disorder (PDD), and mental retardation. On the visual tasks involving closure and spatial memory, the ASD children did not differ from either the verbally matched or non-verbally matched groups. On the face recognition task, however, the ASD group performed significantly below both control groups. These results indicate that, for children with autism, facial identity recognition is specifically impaired in the midst of a normally functioning visual system.

Inversion studies suggest ASD and normally developing populations have divergent strategies for facial identity recognition. While virtually all stimuli are more difficult to recognize upside-down than right-side-up, Yin (1969) showed that inversion disproportionately impairs the recognition of faces relative to the recognition of non-face objects (e.g., airplanes, houses). It was suggested that inversion of a face impairs a *configural* strategy, where the processing of the spatial arrangement and relationship of the features is more important than that of the features themselves. Object recognition, on the other hand, employs a *featural* approach more concerned with the individual parts of an object. Featural processing is less vulnerable to inversion effects presumably because the isolated parts are more important for recognition whereas the entire configuration of features must be mentally reorganized before a face is recognized. Hobson, Ouston and Lee (1988) explored these strategic processing paths in adolescents with autism. They asked ASD and non-ASD adolescents to recognize expression and identity in upright and inverted photographed faces. Although the autism group, like the control group, had difficulty matching inverted faces according to facial expression, it was *superior* when matching the identity of the inverted faces. These findings suggest that individuals with autism do not adopt a configural strategy when recognizing faces, but rely on a more object-based, featural approach. Hence, the cognitive operations that distinguish faces from objects in normal populations may not be as clear-cut for individuals with autism.

Other evidence indicates that the facial features individuals with autism use to pinpoint an identity are different from the features used by the general population. Langdell (1978) asked children with autism and control participants to recognize the photographed faces of their peers presented in either full view or partially masked conditions. In the masked condition, the control children relied more on the eye features whereas children with autism recognized faces primarily by the mouth. In another study, both children with autism and control participants demonstrated evidence for holistic face recognition in that all of the children recognized a face part better when it was presented in the whole face than when it was presented in isolation (Joseph & Tanaka, 2002). However, normal children showed the largest holistic gains for eye features (i.e., eyes were better recognized in the whole face than in isolation) whereas the ASD children showed the greatest holistic gains for mouth features (i.e., mouths were better recognized in the whole face than in isolation). Finally, investigations of eye movements revealed that children with autism perform more visual saccades and spend longer fixation times looking at the mouth of a face as opposed to the eyes (Klin, Jones, Schultz, Volkmar, & Cohen, in press). Taken together, these results suggest that individuals with autism have modified or even contrasting strategies for facial identity recognition. From the features that command attention and facilitate recall to the manner in which the face is processed, ASD individuals exhibit different methods of face processing.

7.2.3 DOMAIN IIb: Recognition of Facial Expression

Domain IIb of the Hierarchical Face Processing Model focuses on the recognition of facial expression. There is a good deal of research concerning this section of the Hierarchical Face Processing Model, as expression recognition is relatively testable and an especially poignant feature in the disabilities of individuals with autism. It relates directly to communicative properties to be explained in Domain III as it is quite an unusual feeling to receive no response or acknowledgement when offering your warmest smile to a child with autism. Hobson, Ouston, and Lee (1988) tested the ability of children with autism to label schematic and photographic faces according to basic emotional expressions (e.g., happy, sad, disgusted). Compared to age- and IQ-matched normal children and retarded children, the ASD group demonstrated a marked impairment in their ability to select the correct emotion. This inability to grasp the emotional content of a face may not reflect an incapacity to process emotional information; it could instead be the result of a general inattentiveness to facial expression. As a test of this explanation, Weeks and Hobson (1987) asked ASD and non-ASD children to sort faces that varied by sex, emotional expression, and type of hat. Normal children sorted by sex first, followed by emotional expression, and then by type of hat. Children with autism, on the other hand, grouped the pictures by sex, then by type of hat, and finally by expression. Even when two pictures differed only in their facial expressions, many children with autism were reluctant to sort on the expression dimension, but did so if prompted by the experimenter. The diagnostic group presumably sorted the faces according to the categories which were most salient. The contrasting degrees of saliency could reflect the object bias in ASD individuals, a product of the previously noted face avoidance behavior.

At the neuroanatomical level, the amygdala nuclei, a structure located in the medial temporal lobe, has been shown to play a key role in the processing of emotional stimuli (Whalen et al., 1998). Studies of brain-damaged patients demonstrate that bilateral amygdala lesions impair performance on tasks of emotion, such as the recognition of basic facial expressions, while leaving other cognitive abilities relatively intact (Adolphs et al., 2001). Some researchers hypothesize that the social and emotional deficits of autism are linked to amygdala processes (Baron-Cohen et al., 2000). Support for this view comes from neuroimaging studies where, unlike normal control participants, the amygdala was *not* activated for individuals with autism when viewing pictures of fearful faces (Critchley et al., 2000). The amygdala was similarly unengaged when ASD individuals interpreted an eye gaze stimulus with respect to its social information (Baron-Cohen, 1995). Thus, neuroimaging studies have identified possible connections between the behavioral deficits in facial expression processing to breakdowns of amygdala function.

7.2.4 DOMAIN III: Interpreting Social Cues

As discussed in the previous section, Domain I and II skills encompass the fundamental abilities of face processing, such as the detection of faces, identification of expression, and the recognition of identity. However, the pragmatics of everyday face processing demand that people go beyond the surface information of a face in an effort to understand the underlying message of its sender. For example, in the real world, we read a person's eye gaze to decipher what they might be thinking, or we evaluate a person's expression to deduce what they might be feeling. Thus, Domain III of the face processing framework focuses on the interpersonal dynamics of face processing. In other words, how people perceive and apply facial cues in their everyday lives to communicate ideas and emotions to others.

7.2.4.1 Eye Contact

The most basic Domain III skill involves the use of eye contact (i.e., the detection that one's eyes are in mutual contact with another's). As a nonverbal form of communication, eye contact has been shown to have a subtle, yet powerful effect on shaping the nature of social interactions. For adults, eye contact is used to emphasize information to an audience, regulate turn-taking in a conversation, convey intimacy, and exercise social control (Kleinke, 1986). Developmentally, it has been shown that 6-month-old babies will attend to a face looking at them for 2 to 3 times longer than a face that is looking in another direction (Papousek & Papousek, 1979). For the young infant, eye contact serves as an early form of prelinguistic communication with the mother (Ling & Ling, 1974) and is especially important for sharing affective states (Stern, 1985).

While most children begin to use eye contact at an early stage in development, this does not seem to be the case for children with autism. In one retrospective study, 90% of parents reported that their school-aged child with autism frequently avoided eye contact in social situations as an infant (Volkmar, Klin, Siegel, & Szatmari, 1986). Joseph and Tager-Flusberg (1997) found that ASD children attended to the face of their respective mothers for significantly less time than Down syndrome children, and that mothers of ASD children had to use physical prompts or prodding to gain the attention of their child. Other studies suggest that children with autism do not differ from other children in the amount of time spent gazing at others, but do differ in the quality of their eye contact. Dawson, Hill, Spencer, Galpert, and Watson (1990) found that during unstructured play, young children with autism exhibited the same amount of eye contact with their mothers as control children. However, unlike the other children, the mutual gaze of children with autism was less likely to be combined with an appropriate facial expression. This result suggests that children with autism do not employ eye contact as a way to communicate emotion or affect to others.

7.2.4.2 Joint Attention

Sometime after the first six months of life, a child learns to use eye gaze for purposes of joint attention. In this triadic exchange, the child employs eye gaze or pointing cues to direct the caregiver's attention toward an external object or event that is of mutual interest. For example, a young infant will smile at her mother and look at a favorite stuffed animal in an attempt to enlist the mother's gaze and assumed attention to the toy. In a typically developing child, referential looking develops around 6 to 9 months of age (Walden & Ogan, 1988) and referential pointing occurs slightly later around 9 and 12 months (Hannan, 1987).

In contrast, spontaneous displays of joint attention occur later and are far less frequent in children with autism (Lewy & Dawson, 1992). Even when ASD children display behaviors of joint attention, their actions lack many of the qualities typically associated with this form of social communication. Similar to the previous findings on eye contact, the joint attention behaviors of children with autism are often devoid of affect, suggesting these actions do not carry any emotional content for the children (Kasari, Sigman, Mundy, & Yirimiya, 1990). Moreover, the joint behaviors of children with autism are more likely to be of the *protoimperative* type where the purpose of the eye gaze is to recruit the assistance of another to obtain a particular object or goal (Kasari et al., 1990). For example, a young child may look at her caregiver and a computer in order to gain her help in turning it on. The purpose of a *protodeclarative* display of joint attention, on the other hand, is to communicate a shared experience to another person (e.g., showing a caregiver that there is an interesting photograph in a magazine), and it is this type of joint attention that is much less frequently exhibited by ASD children. Thus, when joint attention is employed by children with autism, it is usually for instrumental purposes rather than for purposes of social affiliation.

7.2.4.3 Facial Cues in a Social Context

The final component of Domain III abilities concerns the understanding of facial cues in a social situation. This more advanced form of social cognition requires not only the recognition of the facial expression, but an understanding of the social context in which it occurs.

Not unexpectedly, children with autism are impaired in their ability to identify the appropriate emotion when it is embedded in a social context. In one study by Fein, Lucci, Braverman, and Waterhouse (1992), children diagnosed with PDD or autism were shown scenes with children portrayed in different affect-laden situations (e.g., a child eating an ice cream, a child holding a broken toy). The face of the child in the picture was obscured and participants were asked to identify the facial expression that matched the scene. Participants were also given a visual task in which they matched different views of the same object. Relative to verbal- and non-verbal-matched control participants, children with PDD performed significantly worse on the context-affect task than the visual task. This result suggests that these children may experience difficulties when trying to make sense of emotional situations in the real world.

Such real world events were enacted in an experiment by Sigman and colleagues (1992). In one situation, a child was seated at a small table with an experimenter who was showing the child how to use a wooden toy hammer. During the demonstration, the experimenter pretended to strike her finger with the hammer and displayed facial expressions indicating that she was in a great deal of pain and distress. It was found that the children with autism spent less time looking at the distressed experimenter than normal children or children with mental retardation. In fact, children from the ASD group ignored the distressed signals of the adult altogether and continued to play with the toy without interruption. Thus, even when children with autism experience emotionally laden situations first-hand, they fail to display normal signs of emotional empathy and concern.

7.2.5 *Theoretical Accounts*

Two theoretical accounts have been given for the lack of interest that children with autism have for the emotions and feelings of others. According to a view originally described by Kanner (1943), children with autism "come into the world with an innate inability to form the usual, biologically provided affective contact with people" (p. 250). This approach proposes that impaired affective processing is the defining feature of autism and colors every social/emotional interaction of the child. In face processing, this deficit is manifested in the child's lack of reciprocal eye contact, impaired affective joint attention, and the inability to understand and respond appropriately to affective cues in the social environment. Given that these children have little motivation or desire to interact with people, they fail to encode and respond to the affective cues displayed by others. The affective position also assumes that autism is not due to environmental or social influences, but is caused by biological factors. In short, the affective view maintains that social/emotional dysfunction is the root cause of autism whose origins are innately biological.

An alternative view is that children with autism suffer from a cognitive deficit in the development of their "theory of mind." Theory of mind is the human ability to attribute beliefs and mental states to other people. Theory of mind allows a child to think, for example, that their friend Julie likes vanilla ice cream or to infer that their brother does not like his English teacher. While normally developing children acquire a basic understanding of theory of mind by age four, children with autism seem profoundly impaired in their ability to form mental representations for the contents of other people's minds (Volkmar, Carter, Grossman, & Klin, 1997). This deficit is shown by the absence of pretend play where the child must model the cognitions of an imaginary friend, or by failure on false belief tasks where the child must take the mental perspective of another person (Baron-Cohen, Leslie, & Frith, 1985).

An impaired theory of mind hampers these children in social interactions that require an understanding of other people's emotions. Hence, children with autism are less likely to use the protodeclarative form of joint attention because they fail to realize that their emotional state can be shared by others (e.g., being excited about seeing a rainbow is an experience that others will find enjoyable). In distressed situations, children with autism are less likely to demonstrate concern for others because they have little understanding of what a distressed person may be feeling or experiencing. The absence of an awareness of the thoughts and feelings of others would therefore negatively affect inter-personal relations that require social empathy. Thus, in contrast to the affective view, the theory of mind position claims that the social/emotional deficits of autism are not necessarily attributable to the failed understanding of an affective cue, but to the inability to connect one's emotional state to the emotional state of another person.

7.2.6 Summary

In this section, we claim that an important goal of the human face processing system is to facilitate the social communication conveyed through facial cues. To achieve this goal, we propose a face-processing model with three functional stages or domains, each with its separate sub-processing goal (see Figure 1). Domain I abilities are responsible for filtering face stimuli from non-face stimuli. Domain II abilities extract information regarding the identity and expression of the face stimulus. Finally, Domain III abilities emphasize the use of facial information in everyday social communication.

The individual domains are hierarchically ordered such that the successful execution of one domain ability is contingent upon the successful completion of preceding domains. For example, accurate identification of a facial expression (Domain II ability) requires the capacity to selectively attend to faces over other types of non-face objects (Domain I). Similarly, interpretation of a facial expression in a social context (Domain III) requires the recognition of a facial expression in isolation (Domain II). The hierarchical nature of the model also predicts that impairment in one domain will have downstream effects on other processing domains. So, for example, damage to the face selective mechanisms in Domain I should hamper the Domain II ability to recognize facial identity or expression.

The model has important implications when applied to populations with face processing impairments, such as individuals with autism. As reviewed in the chapter, the neurological and behavioral evidence suggests that children with autism experience difficulties in all three processing domains. Domain I deficits are exhibited in ASD individuals behaviorally by face avoidance and neurologically by the failure of faces to activate the fusiform face area. Indicative of their Domain II deficits, individuals with autism also show selective impairment in their ability to recognize the identity and expression of faces. Finally, in their everyday social interactions, children with autism do not make appropriate use of eye gaze and facial cues indicating a deficit in Domain III abilities. Given that damage to earlier processes can have cascading effects on later processes, an important question is the extent to which the Domain I deficit of abnormal fusiform gyrus activity is responsible for the impaired facial recognition and communication found in Domains II and III (Schultz et al., 2000). Note that the converse is equally plausible where autism results in a general disinterest in people which, in turn, causes hypo-activation of the normally face-specific fusiform region. Currently, the causal link between fusiform activity and face perception is uncertain and warrants further investigation.

One advantage of the Hierarchical Face Processing Model is that it provides a framework for assessing the range of face processing deficits related to autism. Using the model, assessments can be developed that pinpoint deficits in the different domain levels thereby providing a clearer picture of what face processing abilities are compromised as a result of autism. As discussed in the next section, this model also suggests strategies for intervention.

7.3 *Let's Face It!*: A Computer-Based Intervention for Developing Face Expertise

7.3.1 *Linking Face Recognition and Expert Object Recognition*

The processes of face recognition bear a striking similarity to the processes associated with expert object recognition (Tanaka, 2001). Like "expert" face recognition, expert object recognition, such as bird watching or dog judging, requires the quick and accurate identification of objects at a specific level of abstraction (Tanaka & Taylor, 1991). For example, just as faces are individuated according to their proper names (e.g., "Bob", "Sue"), expert birdwatchers classify birds according to their specific taxonomic names (e.g., "chipping sparrow"). Moreover, object experts recognize objects in their domain of expertise in terms of a holistic configuration, the same strategy that is employed by the general population when recognizing faces (Gauthier & Tarr, 1997; Gauthier, Williams, Tarr, & Tanaka, 1998). Neurologically, it has been shown that for the expert, objects of expertise trigger that same electrical brain response (Tanaka & Curran, 2001) and engage the same neural substrates (i.e., fusiform gyrus) (Gauthier, Skudlarski, Gore, & Anderson, 2000) as faces. In light of their similarities, it has been suggested that face recognition may not be special in any biological sense, but a general form of perceptual expertise. According to the expertise position, people acquire face expertise as a natural consequence of their extensive exposure to faces and the need to individuate faces at specific levels of categorization.

Can expertise be trained in the laboratory? While it has been suggested that it takes several years to become an expert (Diamond & Carey, 1986), recent work (Gauthier, Tarr, Anderson, Skudlarksi, & Gore, 1999) has demonstrated that with proper instruction, normal adults can be trained to be object experts in a relatively brief period. Gauthier and associates (Gauthier & Tarr, 1997; Gauthier et al., 1998) trained participants to recognize artificial objects, known as Greebles. Greebles were constructed such that Greebles of the same category shared the same basic part features arranged in configuration. Participants learned to classify some Greebles as category members, while other Greebles were learned as individuals. After training, it was shown that for the Greebles learned as individuals, Greeble recognition, like face recognition, relied on configural processing. Brain imaging results also revealed that as participants became experts in Greeble recognition, they demonstrated increased activation in the fusiform face area. Therefore, the fusiform gyrus may not be a face area *per se*, but a brain area that is recruited to perform visual tasks related to perceptual expertise.

Laboratory training of expertise also appears to generalize to the learning of new objects in novel situations (Gauthier et al., 1998; Tanaka & Weiskopf, 2002). In a recent study, Tanaka & Weiskopf (2002) trained participants to individuate wading birds (or owls) at the species level and classify owls (or wading birds) at the family level. After training, it was found that participants were better at discriminating new exemplars of birds that were learned at the species level than new exemplars of birds learned at the family level which suggests that specific categorization is an important element of perceptual expertise. Moreover, the expertise advantage transferred to the discrimination of new species of owls (or wading birds) that were not included in the original training set. Hence, not only are familiar objects more easily recognized as a result of perceptual expertise, but new objects are more easily learned as well.

The studies on laboratory-trained experts make several important points. First, expertise entails the individuation of objects at specific levels of categorization. Second, using this approach, normal adult subjects can achieve expert levels of performance in a relatively short period of time. Third, similar brain areas and cognitive processes are engaged during expert object and face recognition. Finally, expert functioning is not limited to the privileged processing of a few objects found in the training set, but generalizes to the larger class of objects in the expert category.

7.3.2 The Let's Face It! *Program: Computer-Based Face Training for ASD Children*

Given that individuals with autism are selectively impaired in their ability to process facial information, an important question is whether face recognition abilities can be taught through direct instruction and training. That is, can the same strategies and principles that were used to teach Greeble and bird recognition to adults be applied to teach face recognition to children with autism? Toward that goal, we developed the *Let's Face It!* software program, a computer-based curriculum intended to teach children with ASD basic face processing skills.

It is important to stress that the *Let's Face It!* program is not meant to be a substitute for human interaction. However, for ASD populations, there are several advantages to a computer-based approach. First, children with autism may actually benefit more from computer-based instruction than traditional methods (Heimann et al., 1995). Moore and Calvert (2000) compared computer- versus teacher-based approaches in object naming skills. They found that children in the computer-based instruction learned significantly more new words and showed greater motivation for learning activity than children in the traditional teacher-based approach. The features, such as music, variable-tone intensity, character vocalizations, and dynamic animations, are particularly motivating and reinforcing for persons with ASD and can easily be incorporated into computer-based instruction (Ferrari & Harris, 1981; Gutierrez-Griep, 1984). Finally, a computer-based curriculum offers a way to provide cost-effective instruction to ASD children in either a home or school setting.

The *Let's Face It!* program is designed as a suite of interactive games with each game developed to teach a specific face processing skill. The program opens with a startup screen where the child types in his or her name which is used to store game logs and preference information. After the startup screen, the main menu appears displaying the game choices. The program follows the hierarchical stages described by the theoretical Hierarchical Face Processing Model (Figure 1). At the beginning level, the child learns to distinguish faces from non-face objects (Domain I). Once these skills are mastered, the child progresses to games involving the recognition of facial identity (Domain IIa) and facial emotion (Domain IIb). The more advanced games require the child to interpret the meaning of facial cues in a social context (Domain III). By playing the suite of games in the *Let's Face It!* program, the child will receive instruction and practice across a broad range of face processing skills. A representative game from each of the four processing domains is described below.

7.3.2.1 *Example of Domain I Game:* Find a Face

Domain I skills focus on the ability to differentiate faces from other non-face objects. Given that children with autism may have difficulty in selectively attending to faces over other types of objects (Swettenham et al., 1998), the *Find a Face* game encourages face attention abilities. In this game, as shown in Figure 2, faces are camouflaged in a realistic scene and the child's task is to locate the hidden faces with the mouse as quickly as possible. Points are awarded according to the speed with which the faces are located. For the advanced levels of the game, the child must differentiate between hidden faces and a contrast category of hidden objects (e.g., dogs, birds, chairs).

Figure 2. Screenshot of *Find a Face* game where the child finds faces and other target objects hidden in a scene.

7.3.2.2 *Example of Domain IIa Game:* Zap It!

Domain IIa games emphasize the ability to recognize facial identity – a skill that is often compromised in children with autism (Boucher & Lewis, 1992; Klin et al., 1999). In the game *Zap It!* (see Figure 3), the goal is to remove face tokens from the playing field by grouping them with other face tokens in groups of three's according to their identities. Scores accumulate by the number of face tokens that are removed from the playing field. The game ends when the player successfully clears the playing field or when the playing field is completely filled with face tokens. Advanced levels of *Zap It!* require that faces are grouped across changes in facial expression.

7.3.2.3 *Example of Domain IIb Game:* EmotionMaker

Games included in this domain emphasize the ability to recognize facial expressions. In *EmotionMaker*, the child is asked to recreate a target expression from a palette of eyes and mouth features conveying different facial expressions (see Figure 4). As the cursor is dragged over the feature, the child will hear the corresponding verbal label for the feature (e.g., when the cursor is over the sad eyes, he or she will hear the word "sad"). The expression is reconstructed by placing the cursor over the desired feature and clicking the mouse. The goal of *EmotionMaker* is to encourage the processing of facial expressions in terms of their features and configuration. In the advanced level, the child must reconstruct a target expression from its verbal label without the aid of auditory feedback from the features. In *EmotionMaker*, the child is required to attend to both the featural and configural aspects of facial expressions. Pertinent to expression recognition deficits found in children with ASD (Hobson et al., 1988), the game also emphasizes how subtle changes in eye information can alter the perception of the facial expression.

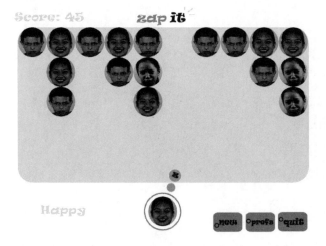

Figure 3. Screenshot of *Zap It!* game where the goal is to form a group of three faces that are similar in facial identity by shooting face tokens with a launcher.

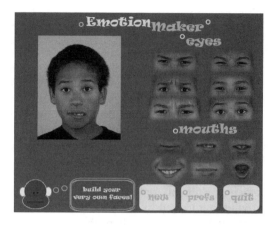

Figure 4. Screenshot of *EmotionMaker* game where the child reconstructs a target emotion from a selection of facial features.

7.3.2.4 Example of Domain III Game: The Eyes Have It

As discussed in a previous section, children with autism have problems interpreting a person's gaze to an external object or event (Kasari et al., 1990). As shown in Fig. 5, *The Eyes Have It* game provides the child with practice in this Domain III ability of joint attention. In this game, a central face is surrounded by a circular array of objects. The eyes of the face are gazing at one of the objects and the child is asked to indicate the object by clicking on it. If the child is correct, the corresponding object sound is played (e.g., a dog barks, a guitar is strummed). If the child is incorrect, a neutral feedback sound is played. Points are awarded depending on the speed and accuracy with which the child makes his or her responses. In the advanced level of the game, the child is asked to identify the object of joint attention in a complex scene.

Figure 5. Sample of *The Eyes Have It* game where the goal is to click on the object that is the focus of the child's eye gaze.

7.3.3 Using Let's Face It! for Assessment and Intervention

The *Let's Face It!* program has practical applications for the assessment and treatment of face processing deficits related to autism. As a diagnostic instrument, the program will help the clinician, teacher, or parent to identify areas where the child may have deficiencies in their face processing abilities; whether it is in their attention to faces (Domain I), recognition of facial identity (Domain IIa) or expression (Domain IIb), or in their interpretation of facial cues (Domain III). As an intervention tool, the hierarchical structure of *Let's Face It!* provides a practical curriculum for teaching face processing abilities across the different skill domains. Within a domain, the difficulty levels of the games are graded so that as the child becomes more proficient with a particular skill, his or her abilities are increasingly challenged. Because all game activities are logged by the program, the child's performance can be continually monitored and evaluated. In short, the *Let's Face It!* program should be useful for both the diagnosis and treatment of face processing deficits.

7.4 Chapter Summary

In this chapter, we claim that normal face processing requires four essential operations – attention to faces, recognition of facial identity, recognition of facial emotion, and interpretation of facial cues. In our model, these operations are hierarchically organized into separate processing domains through which different types of information are abstracted from the face stimulus. A large body of behavioral and neurobiological evidence affirms the importance of these domains for normal face processing, and the growing literature suggests that many of these processes are compromised in ASD individuals.

What is the best way to provide face-processing skills to these individuals? If face recognition is a kind of expertise, it should be possible to develop a training program to teach face-processing skills to children with autism. With this goal in mind, we designed the computer-based program *Let's Face It!* to improve face processing abilities. The ultimate goal of the *Let's Face It!* program is to enhance the social lives of children with autism by providing them with basic face processing skills.

Acknowledgements

We are grateful to Kathy Koenig, Bob Schultz and other members of the Perceptual Expertise Network for their helpful suggestions and ideas. This work is supported by the James S. McDonnell Foundation and grants from the National Science Foundation (#9729030 and #0078745).

References

Adolphs, R., Sears, L., & Piven, J. (2001). Abnormal processing of social information from faces in autism. *Journal of Cognitive Neuroscience, 13*, 232-240.

American Psychiatric Association (1994). *Diagnostic and statistical manual of mental disorders.* Washington, DC: American Psychiatric Association.

Baron-Cohen, S. (1995). *Mindblindness: An essay on autism and theory.* Cambridge, MA: MIT Press.

Baron-Cohen, S., Leslie, A. M., & Frith, U. (1985). Does the autistic child have a "theory of mind"? *Cognition, 21*, 37-46.

Baron-Cohen, S., Ring, H. A., Bullmore, E. T., Wheelwright, S., Ashwin, C., & Williams, S. C. R. (2000). The amygdala theory of autism. *Neuroscience and Biobehavioral Reviews, 24*, 355-364.

Blair, R. J. R., Frith, U., Smith, N., Abell, F., & Cipolotti, L. (2002). Fractionation of visual memory: Agency detection and its impairment in autism. *Neuropsychologia, 108-118.*

Boucher, J., & Lewis, V. (1992). Unfamiliar face recognition in relatively able autistic children. *Journal of Child Psychology and Psychiatry, 33*, 843-859.

Bushnell, I. W. R., Sai, F., & Mullin, J. T. (1989). Neonatal recognition of the mother's face. *British Journal of Developmental Psychology, 7*, 3-15.

Carey, S., Diamond, R., & Woods, B. (1980). The development of face recognition - a maturational component? *Developmental Psychology, 16*, 257-269.

Critchley, H. D., Daly, E. M., Bullmore, E. T., Williams, S. C. R., Van Amelsvoort, T., Robertson, D. M., Rowe, A., Phillips, M., McAlonan, G., Howlin, P., & Murphy, D. G. M. (2000). The functional neuroanatomy of social behaviour: Changes in cerebral blood flow when people with autistic disorder process facial expressions. *Brain, 123*, 2203-2212.

Dawson, G., Hill, D., Spencer, A., Galpert, L., & Watson, L. (1990). Affective exchanges between young autistic children and their mothers. *Journal of Abnormal Child Psychology, 18*, 335-345.

Diamond, R., & Carey, S. (1986). Why faces are not special: An effect of expertise. *Journal of Experimental Psychology: General, 115*, 107-117.

Fantz, R. L. (1963). Pattern vision in newborn infants. *Science, 140*, 296-297.

Fein, D., Lucci, D., Braverman, M., & Waterhouse, L. (1992). Comprehension of affect in context in children with pervasive developmental disorders. *Journal of Child Psychology and Psychiatry, 33*, 1157-1167.

Ferrari, M., & Harris, S. (1981). The limits and motivating potential of sensory stimuli as reinforcers for autistic children. *Journal of Applied Behavioral Analysis, 14*, 339-343.

Gauthier, I., Skudlarski, P., Gore, J., & Anderson, A. (2000). Expertise for cars and birds recruits brain areas involved in face recognition. *Nature Neuroscience, 3*, 191-197.

Gauthier, I., & Tarr, M. J. (1997). Becoming a 'Greeble' expert: Exploring the face recognition mechanism. *Vision Research, 37*, 1673-1682.

Gauthier, I., Tarr, M. J., Anderson, A. W., Skudlarksi, P., & Gore, J. C. (1999). Activation of the middle fusiform "face area" increases with expertise in recognizing novel objects. *Nature Neuroscience, 2*, 568-573.

Gauthier, I., Williams, P., Tarr, M. J., & Tanaka, J. W. (1998). Training "Greeble" experts: A framework for studying expert object recognition processes. *Vision Research, 38*, 2401-2428.

Gutierrez-Griep, R. (1984). Student preferences of sensory reinforcers. *Education and Training of Mentally Retarded, 19*, 108-113.

Hannan, T. (1987). A cross-sequential assessment of the occurrences of pointing in 3- to 12-month-old human infants. *Infant Behavior and Development, 10*, 11-22.

Hauck, M., Fein, D., & Maltby, N. (1999). Memory for faces in children with autism. *Child Neuropsychology, 4*, 187-198.

Heimann, M., Nelson, K., Tjus, T., & Gillberg, C. (1995). Increasing reading and communication skills in children with autism through an interactive multi-media computer program. *Journal of Autism and Developmental Disorders, 25*, 459-480.

Hobson, R., Ouston, J., & Lee, A. (1988). What's in a face? The case of autism. *British Journal of Psychology, 79*(4), 441-453.

Joseph, R., & Tanaka, J. W. (2002). Holistic and part-based recognition in children with autism. *Journal of Child Psychiatry and Psychology, 43*, 1-14.

Joseph, R. M., & Tager-Flusberg, H. (1997). An investigation of attention and affect in children with autism and Down syndrome. *Journal of Autism & Developmental Disorders, 27*, 385-396.

Kanner, L. (1943). Autistic disturbances of affective contact. *Nervous Child, 2*, 227-250.

Kanwisher, N., McDermott, J., & Chun, M. M. (1997). The fusiform face area: A module in human extrastriate cortex specialized for face perception. *Journal of Neuroscience, 17*, 4302-4311.

Kasari, C., Sigman, M., Mundy, P., & Yirimiya, N. (1990). Affective sharing in the context of joint attention interactions of normal, autistic and mentally retarded children. *Journal of Autism and Developmental Disorders, 20*, 87-100.

Kleinke, C. L. (1986). Gaze and eye contact: A research review. *Psychological Bulletin, 100*, 78-100.

Klin, A., Jones, W., Schultz, R., Volkmar, F. R., & Cohen, D. J. (in press). Visual fixation patterns during viewing of natural social situations as predictors of social competence in individuals with autism. *Archives of General Psychiatry, 59*, 809-816.

Klin, A., Sparrow, S. S., de Bildt, A., Cicchetti, D. V., Cohen, D. J., & Volkmar, F. R. (1999). A normed study of face recognition in autism and related disorders. *Journal of Autism and Developmental Disorders, 29*, 499-508.

Langdell, T. (1978). Recognition of faces: An approach to the study of autism. *Journal of Psychology and Psychiatry, 19*, 255-268.

Lewy, A. L., & Dawson, G. (1992). Social stimulation and joint attention in young autistic children. *Journal of Abnormal Child Psychology, 20*, 555-566.

Ling, D., & Ling, A. H. (1974). Communication development in the first three years of life. *Journal of Speech and Hearing Research, 17*, 146-159.

Moore, M. & Calvert, S. (2000). Brief report: Vocabulary acquisition for children with autism: Teacher or computer instruction. *Journal of Autism and Developmental Disorders, 30*, 359-362.

Morton, J., & Johnson, M. (1991). CONSPEC and CONLERN: A two-process theory of infant face recognition. *Psychological Review, 98*, 164-181.

Osterling, J., & Dawson, G. (1994). Early recognition of children with autism: A study of first birthday home videotapes. *Journal of Autism and Developmental Disorders, 24*, 247-257.

Papousek, H., & Papousek, M. (1979). Early ontogeny of human social interaction: Its biological roots and social dimensions. In M. v. Cranach (Ed.), *Human Ethology: Claims and limits of a new discipline* (pp. 456-478). Cambridge, MA: Cambridge University Press.

Pascalis, O., de Schonen, S., Morton, J., Deruelle, C., & Fabre-Grenet, M. (1995). Mother's face recognition by neonates: A replication and an extension. *Infant Behavior and Development, 18*, 79-85.

Schultz, R. T., Gauthier, I., Klin, A., Fulbright, R. K., Anderson, A. W., Volkmar, F., Skudlarski, P., Lacadie, C., Cohen, D. J., & Gore, J. C. (2000). Abnormal ventral temporal cortical activity during face discrimination among individuals with autism and Asperger Syndrome. *Archives of General Psychiatry, 57*, 331-340.

Sigman, M. D., Kasari, C., Kwon, J. H., & Yirmiya, N. (1992). Responses to the negative emotions of others by autistic, mentally retarded, and normal children. *Child Development, 63*, 796-807.

Stern, D. (1985). *The interpersonal world of the human infant.* New York: Basic Books.

Swettenham, J., Baron-Cohen, S., Charman, T., Cox, A., Baird, G., Drew, A., Rees, L., & Wheelwright, S. (1998). The frequency and distribution of spontaneous attention shifts between social and nonsocial stimuli in autistic, typically developing, and nonautistic developmentally delayed infants. *Journal of Child Psychology and Psychiatry, 39*, 747-753.

Tanaka, J. W. (2001). The entry point of face recognition: Evidence for face expertise. *Journal of Experimental Psychology: General, 130*, 534-543.

Tanaka, J. W., & Curran, T. (2001). The neural basis of expert object recognition. *Psychological Science, 12 (1)*, 43-47.

Tanaka, J. W., & Taylor, M. (1991). Object categories and expertise: Is the basic level in the eye of the beholder? *Cognitive Psychology, 23*, 457-482.

Tanaka, J. W., & Weiskopf, D. (2002). Perceptual expertise and bird recognition. Manuscript in preparation.

Volkmar, F., Carter, A., Grossman, J., & Klin, A. (1997). Social development in autism. In D. J. Cohen & F. R. Volkmar (Eds.), *Handbook of autism and pervasive developmental disorders* (pp. 173-194). New York: John Wiley & Sons.

Volkmar, F. R., Klin, A., Siegel, B., & Szatmari, P. (1986). An evaluation of DSM-III criteria for infantile autism. *Journal of the American Academy of Child Psychiatry, 25*, 190-197.

Walden, T., & Ogan, T. (1988). The development of social referencing. *Child Development, 59*, 1230-1240.

Weeks, J. S., & Hobson, P. R. (1987). The salience of facial expression for autistic children. *Journal of Child Psychology & Psychiatry & Allied Disciplines, 28*, 137-151.

Whalen, P. J., Rauch, S. L., Etcoff, N. L., McInerney, S. C., Lee, M. B., & Jenike, M. A. (1998). Masked presentations of emotional facial expressions modulate amygdala activity without explicit knowledge. *The Journal of Neuroscience, 18*, 411-418.

Yin, R. (1969). Looking at upside-down faces. *Journal of Experimental Psychology, 81*, 141-145.

Address for Correspondence

James W. Tanaka
Department of Psychology
Severance Lab
Oberlin College
Oberlin, OH 44074
USA
E-mail: tanaka@cs.oberlin.edu

Face Processing and Person Processing: Are They Both the Same?

Katja Seitz

8.1 Introduction

Literature on face processing sometimes uses the term 'person' as equivalent to the term 'face,' not clearly distinguishing between the two. This is true even though everyone knows that the face is only one part of an entire person – no doubt the most important part for social interaction – but still just one part. It seems reasonable to ask for a more careful use of the two terms. The term 'person' should be used in visual processing studies where the entire person from head to toe is involved and the term 'person processing' should be adopted for research in this field. If this distinction is taken into account, it becomes apparent that up to now experimental research has focused on the development of face processing. Person processing as defined above has only been studied within the applied research field of eyewitness testimony (in adults: Cutler, Penrod, & Martens, 1987; Lindsay, Wallbridge, & Drennan, 1987; Narby, Cutler, & Penrod, 1996; Thomson, Robertson, & Vogt, 1982; in children: King & Yuille, 1987; Marin, Holmes, Guth, & Kovac, 1979; Parker & Carranza, 1989; Roebers & Lockl, 1999). However, this field of research is not predominantly concerned with person recognition. It is just one area of interest in eyewitness research and not even the main one. Eyewitness research only studies person recognition performance, i.e., the outcome of information processing. In contrast, experimental face research focuses on different modes of processing.

The different research interests of face processing and person recognition consequently lead to the use of different types of research methods. Research in face processing mostly uses realistic photos of faces, but also drawings of faces, and varies them during presentation with the aim of producing certain patterns of response. Eyewitness researchers attempt to create ecologically valid settings and therefore use real people, realistic photos or video-films of individuals. Conditions are mainly varied in the encoding and recognition phases.

For both theoretical and methodological reasons, a direct comparison of face and person processing is not yet possible from a developmental point of view. However, there have been a few attempts to deal with aspects of face and person processing within a single article.

8.2 Previous Comparisons of Information Processing with Face and Person Stimuli

Apart from an integrative review entitled "Face-recognition memory: Implications for children's eyewitness testimony" written by Chance and Goldstein (1984), only two empirical studies have been concerned with face and person processing (Downing, Jiang, Shuman, & Kanwisher, 2001; Soppe, 1986) up to now. Chance and Goldstein (1984) aim to derive implications from face recognition memory research for children's eyewitness performance. The developmental data is taken from ten laboratory studies on face recognition and two studies within the eyewitness context. Based also on the somewhat more extensive literature on adults' recognition performance, the authors' conclusion consists of suggestions for further "questions for research" and "practical – mainly cautionary – implications for legal practices ..." (Chance & Goldstein, 1984; p. 82). As a direct comparison of face and person processing was not the aim of these authors – instead they focused on personal and situational factors that determine recognition performance – there were no comments on a comparison of these two areas of research.

8.2.1 Soppe's (1986) Work on Face Recognition and Person Identification

Even though Soppe's (1986) article is entitled "Children's recognition of unfamiliar faces: Developments and determinates" whole persons are included as stimuli in a recognition task as well. Soppe tested face recognition by showing a series of ten slides of faces (each for 5 seconds) and – after an interval of 3 minutes – presenting a set of 20 faces, ten that had been seen before and ten new faces. A second recognition task included persons as stimuli in the encoding phase and faces in the recognition phase. Within this person recognition task, subjects were unexpectedly confronted with two series of eight pictures, each series showing the face of one of two persons who they had met briefly three days earlier. The persons were present for 105 seconds and they also talked to the subject in the encoding phase. Nearly 300 subjects, 8, 9, 10, 11, 12, and 13 years old, participated in the study. All subjects carried out both recognition tasks. The results clearly indicated two different developmental patterns for the two tasks. There was no correlation between the two recognition scores. Person recognition performance did not change between the ages of 8 and 11, but decreased at age 12 and reached the level of the 8- and 11-year-olds again at age 13. Face recognition performance of photographs remained stable between the ages of 8 and 12 and increased at the age of 13. Overall, face recognition showed a general age effect whereas person recognition did not. Therefore, person recognition performance is less dependent on the age of the child than face recognition performance.

8.2.2 A Neuro-Imaging Study on Face and Person Processing

Downing, Jiang, Shuman, and Kanwisher (2001) recently presented a series of functional magnetic resonance imaging (fMRI) studies in which various visual stimuli were viewed by adult subjects while these were scanned. The stimuli were photographs of mammals, whole objects, faces or bodies of humans, and photographs of parts of bodies or faces of humans. Line drawings, silhouettes and stick figures were also presented. The authors found a region in the right lateral occipitotemporal cortex that produced a significantly stronger response when the subjects viewed photographs of bodies or parts of bodies of humans than when they viewed various other pictures. This "extrastriate body area" (EBA), as Downing and colleagues named it provisionally, responded strongly to whole bodies and parts of the body of humans including parts of the face but not to whole faces and other objects. The activation in the EBA was stronger for parts of the body than for parts of other objects. The authors conclude that the EBA reflects a specialized neural system for the visual perception of human bodies and body parts, with the exception of whole faces.

8.2.3 Remarks on Previous Comparisons

Soppe's study (1986) employs two different methods for face and person recognition, and the Downing et al. (2001) report is restricted to adults. As evidence on face and person processing is quite small so far, it does not allow a conclusion on the relation between both subjects. However, these studies indicate that there may be some differences between face and person processing. As Soppe's (1986) findings suggest, the developmental courses of face and person recognition performance may differ. But there may also be differences in the mode of processing visual face and person stimuli. Precisely this lack of knowledge on the differences and similarities in the course of the development of face and person processing raises the question that heads this chapter.

The remainder of this chapter will attempt to answer this question. The first part of the chapter (Section 8.3) outlines the development of the ability to recognize face and person stimuli. The underlying processes of face and person recognition are then explained in the next section (Section 8.4), and in the last section (Section 8.5) an attempt is made to integrate findings from different studies examining whether face and person processing are identical. These findings are discussed in the light of the debate on face-specific mechanisms.

The entire chapter focuses on the age-range of 4-year-old preschoolers to adults. Since the main interest here is face and person processing of unfamiliar faces and persons, literature on the processing of familiar faces (Bruce & Young, 1986; Burton, Bruce, & Johnston, 1990) is not cited.

8.3 The Developmental Course of Face and Person Recognition Performance

8.3.1 Previous Studies on Face Recognition and Person Recognition

As the age range of interest in the present chapter lies between preschool age and adulthood and therefore overlaps with the Chapters 4 and 5, a complete description of the developmental literature on face processing for this age-range is superfluous here. Face recognition performance increases from age 6 to 10 (for an overview see Chung & Thomson, 1995; Carey, 1996; Chapter 4). This age effect is very robust, the evidence for it is enormous and it is an effect that is not discussed controversially. The development of face recognition performance between the age of 10 and adulthood sometimes shows a dip (Carey, Diamond, & Woods, 1980) and sometimes reveals a plateau (Diamond & Carey, 1977; for an overview see Chapter 5).

Evidence on the development of whole person recognition performance is far from clear. Applied research studies on person identification in children (and adults) vary in many aspects and are therefore hardly comparable. For example, the person to be recognized may have been seen before on a slide (Parker & Carranza, 1989), or have taken part in a video (Yarmey, 1988), a staged incident (Brigham, Van Verst, & Bothwell, 1986) or even a personal interaction with the subject (Davies, Tarrant, & Flin, 1989). In addition to the directness of target presentation, the time allowed to encode the stimulus varies from a few seconds (Parker & Carranza, 1989) to over 5 minutes (Davies, Tarrant, & Flin, 1989). Even more heterogeneous is the retention interval. In some studies an immediate recognition test was carried out (Parker & Carranza, 1989), while others measured recognition weeks after the encoding phase (Davies, Stevenson-Robb, & Flin, 1988). The recognition test itself may consist of an array, i.e., a simultaneous presentation of different persons, or a sequential presentation, i.e., one person at a time. The number of distractors (persons who were not seen and therefore should not be identified) is another source of variance (from one to more than a dozen).

Whether a recognition test is constructed with the possible absence of the person to be recognized (target absent array) or whether the subjects know that the target is present and that they just have to choose it (target present array), is an important difference, too, especially from a developmental point of view. There tends to be an age related increase in person recognition performance under target absent conditions (for an overview see Davies, 1993, see also Chapter 9). However, there is also some evidence contradicting this indication: Studies carried out by Baenninger (1994) and Davies (1993) could not find an age effect in recognition performance when the targets were not present in recognition arrays, so it seems that target absent arrays per se cannot produce age related differences in identification performance.

All in all, it is impossible to draw a single conclusive picture for the developmental course of person recognition on the basis of the evidence provided by applied research on eyewitness identification. Heterogeneous methodological approaches find an age related increase in person identification on the one hand, but also 6-year-old children showing person identification performances comparable to those of 10-year-old children or even adults on the other.

As described above, literature on face processing is homogeneous with regard to the developmental course of face recognition performance from age 6 to 10. Since applied research cannot provide a uniform picture of person recognition in the course of development – mostly due to methodological variations – a comparison of both recognition performances is not yet possible. In order to compare the developmental course of face and person recognition directly, the same methodological approach should be used for both faces and whole persons.

8.3.2 A Direct Comparison of Face and Person Recognition

The initial study on a direct comparison of the development of face and person recognition performance employed a short-term recognition task (typical for experimental research in face processing, Diamond & Carey, 1977) with pictures of faces and whole persons presented to children from 3 to 10 years of age and adults. When confronted with either a grayscale photo of a face or a black and white photo of a whole person for five seconds and asked to identify the face or person immediately from a four-alternative array, 4-, 6-, 8-, 10-year-olds, and adults showed similar recognition performances for both photos of persons and photos of faces (Seitz, Limmer, & Schumann-Hengsteler, 1999; Seitz & Schumann-Hengsteler, 1999). Only the 3-year-olds revealed a contrasting pattern of results: they did much better in person than in face recognition. Overall, an age effect could be observed, i.e., an increase of face and person recognition performance with age. Several other unpublished studies used the same material and found absolutely identical result patterns with regard to the developmental increase in face and person recognition from the age of 6 years onwards. Another series of experiments studied the effects of changes in posture and clothing on the development of unfamiliar person recognition (Seitz, in press). The increase of person recognition from the age of 4 years onwards was supported again. Therefore the age effect in person recognition is reliable and robust, just as it is in face recognition. Figure 1 illustrates the developmental course for face and person recognition from 6 years to adulthood. The plotted recognition performance is averaged across three yet unpublished studies and the data from Seitz and Schumann-Hengsteler (1999). All of these studies used the same face and person material in a short-term recognition paradigm similar to the one described above. The black dots show the data points for face recognition reported by Carey (1996). The overall performance level differs because Carey's recognition tasks involved conditions in which the targets were disguised or at least manipulated. As the figure shows, the performance level in each age group is identical for face and person recognition when the same method is employed. Moreover, apart from the level of performance, our data match Carey's data almost perfectly.

However, there were differences in recognition performance between faces and persons when the short-term recognition task described above was used: 3-year-old children showed better recognition performance in the whole person condition than in the face condition (Seitz & Schumann-Hengsteler, 1999). Additional evidence indicating that person recognition is easier than face recognition was found in a study employing a different method: target absent options were included in the recognition array. Here 6-year-olds and to some extent, 8-year-olds showed a pattern of results similar to the 3-year-olds in the initial study under target present conditions (Seitz, Limmer, & Schumann-Hengsteler, 1999): Accuracy in person recognition was higher compared to face recognition.

All in all, on the basis of this evidence, a description of the developmental course of face and person recognition performances leads to the conclusion that performance is similar when the same method is used. However, if differences occur, it is always person recognition that outperforms face recognition.

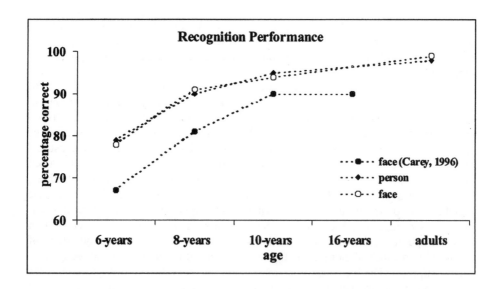

Figure 1. Developmental courses for face and person recognition performances.

8.4 Development of Modes of Face and Person Processing

8.4.1 Previous Findings on the Mode of Face Processing

The most popular explanation for the improvement in face processing between the ages of 6 and 10 years is the acquisition of face-specific expertise relevant for face encoding (Carey, 1996; Carey & Diamond, 1994; Diamond & Carey, 1986). Earlier assumptions of a developmental shift away from the use of featural facial information (e.g., the mouth) to the use of configural facial information (the distance between two features, e.g., the mouth-nose-distance) in face recognition have been modified (Carey & Diamond, 1977; Carey & Diamond, 1994; Diamond & Carey, 1977). It has been shown that from the age of 6 years onwards children use configural information of a newly presented face, just as older children and adults do (Carey & Diamond, 1994). The difference between younger children's facial encoding and that of adults lies in another source of information, the "second order relational information" (Carey, 1996). This source of information is acquired by norm-based encoding. While gathering experience with faces an internal representation of a norm-face is formed and elaborated upon. Since a new face is encoded in relation to the internal norm-face, recognition performance increases with the elaboration of the norm. This constitutes the expertise-factor (Carey, 1996; Carey & Diamond, 1994). Evidence supporting the expertise-thesis comes from short-term recognition tasks with upright and inverted faces as well as from face composite studies (Carey & Diamond, 1994; Diamond & Carey, 1986; Leder & Bruce, 2000).

Additional evidence for children's access to information other than featural information in face processing comes from Tanaka, Kay, Grinnell, Stansfield, and Szechter's (1998) study with 6-, 8-, and 10-year-olds using the part-whole paradigm. This paradigm is used to assess whether there is a complete over part probe advantage (CPA, Donnelly & Davidoff, 1999) in face recognition. A whole face is presented in the encoding phase, and in the test phase the recognition array consists of the identical face and a second face in which one feature (either the eyes, nose or mouth) has been replaced by a new feature (e.g., the familiar eyes have been replaced by new eyes). This whole face recognition condition is contrasted with a test condition in which only two isolated features (either the eyes, nose, or mouth) are shown. One is the original feature that was seen in the context of the face during the encoding phase and the other is a new, previously unseen feature (e.g., familiar nose vs. new nose). If faces are encoded on the basis of features, then recognition performance should not differ in both conditions because it is the feature that leads to the correct recognition of the face. If faces are processed more configurally, then the whole face condition should lead to higher performance than the isolated part condition. Tanaka et al. (1998) found that 6-, 8-, and 10-year-old children are better at the recognition of facial features if additional context information is provided in the recognition test. 6-year-old children (as well as adults, Tanaka & Farah, 1993) use a configural encoding strategy in face recognition tasks.

8.4.2 *The Part-Whole Paradigm in Person Processing*

Exactly what kind of facial information is used in different face processing tasks is of great interest from a developmental point of view. Just as different types of information might be used in face processing, person processing might also rely on feature-based or analytical encoding strategies (Diamond & Carey, 1977; Schwarzer, 1997, 2000; Schwarzer & Korell, 2001) or, in contrast, relational or holistic encoding strategies (Carey & Diamond, 1994; Tanaka et al., 1998). Like faces, whole persons represent a class of stimuli that is determined by a fixed configuration of elements (e.g., the head is attached to the upper part of the torso, the legs are attached below the left and right side of the torso). Isolated elements like arms or legs are person features. To test whether persons are processed like faces, i.e., more holistically, the part-whole paradigm introduced by Tanaka and Farah (1993; Tanaka et al., 1998) is adopted to study person recognition processes. To answer our initial question (Are face and person processing both the same?) the two object classes are compared (Seitz, 2002). The part-whole paradigm is implemented as a short-term recognition test in which a complete face or a complete person is presented in the encoding phase followed in the recognition phase by either two complete faces/persons or only isolated features of the stimuli (for examples see Figure 2). The critical features in faces are the eyes, nose, and mouth. Critical person features are the arms, torso and legs. In both the complete condition and the isolated part condition, only one feature at a time is critical for correct recognition. If context information aids recognition performance, i.e., if a more configural encoding strategy is used, a complete over part probe advantage should occur. If persons are encoded on the basis of features, results for the isolated part condition and the complete condition should be similar.

The results (see Figure 3) are clear: A comparison of face and person recognition shows that children of 8 and 10 years of age as well as adults process faces and persons in the same way. All subjects benefit from the whole person condition compared to the isolated person condition, i.e., show a CPA in person recognition. Additionally, face recognition conditions produce the same pattern of results. Faces and persons are processed with a more configural encoding strategy. However, featural information is also used by all age groups. This is shown by performance in the isolated part condition. It exceeds chance level, which could not happen if isolated features were not used for the recognition task. Overall performance increased with age for both faces and persons, and for both isolated parts and whole stimuli. (The effect of material – face recognition performance is better than person recognition – is due to the overall difference in the complexity of the material).

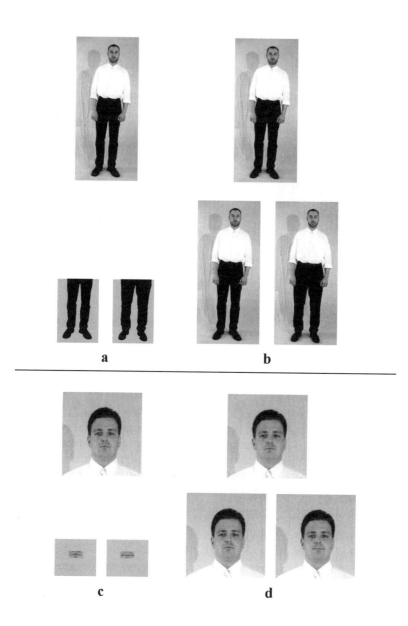

Figure 2. Examples of stimuli from encoding phase (upper section) and recognition phase (lower section) for (a) the isolated part condition for persons, (b) the whole person condition, (c) the isolated part condition for faces, and (d) the whole face condition (Seitz, 2002).

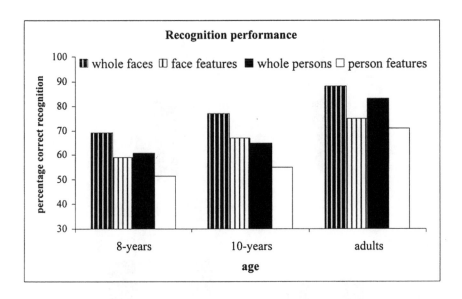

Figure 3. Recognition performance for faces and persons using the part-whole paradigm (means from Experiment 1 and 2 from Seitz, 2002).

8.5 Conclusion

A synthesis of all the reported findings leads us to venture a tentative positive answer to our initial question – Are face and person processing both the same? Since the empirical basis of a direct comparison (using similar material and an identical methodological approach) is still quite small at the moment however, conclusions on the new subject of person processing should be made with some caution.

8.5.1 Recognition Performance

If only one methodology is used, and photos of faces and photos of whole persons are presented in a short-term recognition task, the performance of 4- to 16-year-old children and adults is absolutely identical for both kinds of material (see Figure 1). However, the finding that 3-year-olds show higher recognition accuracy in persons needs further investigation. This is not just a solitary result since an advantage of person recognition over face recognition has also been found in additional studies where the methodology was varied (Seitz, Limmer, & Schumann-Hengsteler, 1999). This conclusion can also be drawn when the studies on person identification (Davies, 1993) and on face recognition (Chung and Thomson, 1995) are compared: When there are differences between face and person recognition performance, results are in favor of person recognition.

Explaining these differences between face and person recognition performance seems easy as far as the overall comparison of findings from both research areas is concerned. Methodological differences definitely account for different findings in person identification studies. However, the methodological argument is not valid in our studies where the same method was used for faces and persons. Here explanations are speculative and should be explored further.

8.5.2 Underlying Processes in Person Recognition

The results obtained with the part-whole paradigm (Tanaka & Farah, 1993; Tanaka et al., 1998) show no reliable differences between the processing of faces and whole persons. Features of both materials – eyes, nose, mouth in faces, and arms, torso, legs in persons – are recognized better by children and adults if additional contextual information is provided in the recognition test (Seitz, 2002). Therefore, the conclusion has to be drawn that face and person processing do not differ. Configural encoding strategies are used by all age groups studied, but feature-based information is encoded as well (Seitz, 2002).

The expertise thesis (Carey & Diamond, 1994; Diamond & Carey, 1986) of face processing assumes that there are two types of configural or relational information. The type studied with the part-whole paradigm must be age-independent configural information, because 8- and 10-year-olds showed the same pattern of results as adults. Whether the expertise thesis can be adopted for person processing, i.e., whether there are two kinds of configural or relational information in persons, is a question for further research. If so, the internal representation of a norm-person, which has developed from experience with persons, would then serve as a model with which every newly encountered person is compared. This hypothesis could very well turn out to be correct. Person-inversion studies could show an age x orientation interaction and so the existence of two types of configural or relational information in whole persons. This would also imply an age- or experience-dependent type of relational information in persons, which could explain a general age-related increase in person recognition performance such as the age effect found in the studies described above.

8.5.3 Face- and Person-Specific Mechanisms

In the 90s the debate on face-exclusive mechanisms had a renaissance. Farah (1996) came up with neuropsychological evidence for face-exclusive mechanisms, and again a discourse on this subject began. Specifically, the work of Gauthier and Tarr (1997; Gauthier, Tarr, Anderson, Skudlarski, & Gore, 1999; Gauthier, Skudlarski, Gore, & Anderson, 2000) and the earlier developmental work of Diamond and Carey (1986) provided empirical evidence for more general but fine-tuned mechanisms that are characterized as processors of homogeneous classes of frequently experienced stimuli. For example, these mechanisms come into play when dog experts process dog stimuli (Diamond & Carey, 1986) or car experts process car stimuli (Gauthier et al., 2000). In line with this argument our data clearly show that at least functionally (not necessarily physiologically, but see Downing et al., 2001; Gauthier et al., 1999, 2000) face and whole person processing do not differ. Put differently: Our findings contradict the face-exclusive mechanism hypothesis. However, Farah and colleagues weakened the idea of face-specific mechanisms themselves (Farah, Tanaka, & Drain, 1995; Farah, Wilson, Drain, & Tanaka, 1998). Results from comparative studies on the processing of faces, houses and words led them to assume that it is not the kind of representation used for various materials that differs, but rather the degree to which certain representations are used for different materials (Farah, Wilson, Drain, & Tanaka, 1998). Holistic representation is required for faces and to a lesser degree for houses, but words are not represented holistically. Feature-based representation is used for words and to a lesser degree for houses, but faces are almost never represented in this way. "...Face recognition differs from other types of pattern recognition in its use of relatively holistic, undecomposed representations" (Farah, Tanaka, & Drain, 1995; p. 634). However, it does not differ from whole person recognition (Seitz, 2002). This is hardly surprising if we think of Gauthier et al.'s (1997) thesis on fine-tuned processes or of Diamond and Carey's (1986) expertise-thesis. Entire persons are normally seen as often as faces during one's life-time (except for passport photographs and psychological studies, where faces are presented in isolation). For this reason, expertise in person processing should be comparable to expertise in face processing. Our results confirm that the mechanisms that aid the processing of faces and persons are similar.

References

Baenninger, M. (1994). The development of face recognition: Featural or configurational processing? *Journal of Experimental Child Psychology, 57*, 377-396.
Brigham, J. C., Van Verst, M., & Bothwell, R. K. (1986). Accuracy of children's eyewitness identifications in a field setting. *Basic & Applied Social Psychology, 7*, 295-306.
Bruce, V., & Young, A. (1986). Understanding face recognition. *British Journal of Psychology, 77*, 305-327.
Burton, A. M., Bruce, V., & Johnston, R. A. (1990). Understanding face recognition with an interactive activation model. *British Journal of Psychology, 81*, 361-380.
Carey, S. (1996). Perceptual classification and expertise. In R. Gelman & T. K. - F. Au (Eds.), *Perceptual and cognitive development* (pp. 49-69). San Diego, CA: Academic Press.
Carey, S., & Diamond, R. (1977). From piecemeal to configurational representation of faces. *Science, 195*, 312-314.
Carey, S., & Diamond, R. (1994). Are faces perceived as configurations more by adults than by children? *Visual Cognition, 1*(2/3), 253-274.
Carey, S., Diamond, R., & Woods, B. (1980). Development of face recognition-a maturational component? *Developmental Psychology, 16*(4), 257 - 269.
Chance, J. E., & Goldstein, A. G. (1984). Face-recognition memory: Implications for children's eyewitness testimony. *Journal of Social Issues, 40*(2), 69-85.
Chung, M. - S., & Thomson, D. M. (1995). Development of face recognition. *British Journal of Psychology, 86*, 55-87.

Cutler, B. L., Penrod, S. D., & Martens, T. K. (1987). Improving the reliability of eyewitness identification. Putting context into context. *Journal of Applied Psychology, 72*(4), 629-637.

Davies, G. M. (1993). Children's memory for other people: An integrative review. In C. Nelson (Ed.), *Memory and affect in development* (Vol. 26, pp. 123-157). Hillsdale, NJ: Lawrence Erlbaum Associates.

Davies, G. M., Stevenson-Robb, Y., & Flin, R. (1988). Tales out of school: Children's memory for an unexpected incident. In M. Gruneberg, P. Morris, & R. Sykes (Eds.), *Practical aspects of memory* (Vol. 1, pp. 122-127). Chichester, UK: Wiley.

Davies, G., Tarrant, A., & Flin, R. (1989). Close encounters of the witness kind: Children's memory for a simulated health inspection. *British Journal of Psychology, 80*, 415-429.

Diamond, R., & Carey, S. (1977). Developmental changes in the representation of faces. *Journal of Experimental Child Psychology, 23*, 1-22.

Diamond, R., & Carey, S. (1986). Why faces are and are not special: An effect of expertise. *Journal of Experimental Psychology: General, 155*(2), 107-117.

Donnelly, N., & Davidoff, J. (1999). The mental representations of faces and houses: Issues concerning parts and wholes. *Visual Cognition, 6*(3/4), 319-343.

Downing, P. E., Jiang, Y., Shuman, M., & Kanwisher, N. (2001). A cortical area selective for visual processing of the human body. *Science, 293*(5539), 2470-2473.

Farah, M. J. (1996). Is face recognition "special"? Evidence from neuropsychology. *Behavioural Brain Research, 76*, 181-189.

Farah, M. J., Tanaka, J. W., & Drain, H. M. (1995). What causes the face inversion effect? *Journal of Experimental Psychology: Human Perception and Performance, 21*(3), 628-634.

Farah, M. J., Wilson, K. D., Drain, M., & Tanaka, J. N. (1998). What is "special" about face perception? *Psychological Review, 105*(3), 482-498.

Gauthier, I., Skudlarski, P., Gore, J. C., & Anderson, A. W. (2000). Expertise for cars and birds recruits brain areas involved in face recognition. *Nature Neuroscience, 3*(2), 191-197.

Gauthier, I., & Tarr, M. J. (1997). Becoming a "greeble" expert: Exploring mechanisms for face recognition. *Vision Research, 37*(12), 1673-1682.

Gauthier, I., Tarr, M. J., Anderson, A. W., Skudlarski, P., & Gore, J. C. (1999). Activation of the middle fusiform "face area" increases with expertise in recognizing novel objects. *Nature Neuroscience, 2*(6), 568-573.

King, M. A., & Yuille, J. C. (1987). Suggestibility in the child witness. In S. J. Ceci, M. P. Toglia, & D. F. Ross (Eds.) *Children's witness memory* (pp. 24-35). New York: Springer.

Leder, H., & Bruce, V. (2000). When inverted faces are recognized: The role of configural information in face recognition. *The Quarterly Journal of Experimental Psychology, 53A*(2), 513-536.

Lindsay, R. C. L., Wallbridge, H., & Drennan, D. (1987). Do the clothes make the man?: An exploration of the effect of lineup attire on eyewitness identification accuracy. *Canadian Journal of Behavioral Science, 19*(4), 463-478.

Marin, B. V., Holmes, D. L., Guth, M., & Kovac, P. (1979). The potential of children as eyewitnesses. *Law and Human Behaviour, 3*(4), 295-306.

Narby, D. J., Cutler, B. L., & Penrod, S. D. (1996). The effects of witness, target, and situational factors on eyewitness identifications. In S. L. Sporer, Malpass, R. S., & Koehnken, G. (Ed.), *Psychological issues on eyewitness identification* (pp. 23-52). Mahwah, NJ: Lawrence Erlbaum Associates.

Parker, J. F., & Carranza, L. E. (1989). Eyewitness testimony of children in target-present and target-absent lineups. *Law and Human Behavior, 13*(2), 133-149.

Roebers, C. M. & Lockl, K. (1999). Der Einfluß von Metakognitionen und vorheriger Irreführung auf die Identifikationsleistung kindlicher Augenzeugen. *Zeitschrift für Entwicklungspsychologie und Pädagogische Psychologie, 31*(3), 116-126.

Schwarzer, G. (1997). Kategorisierung von Gesichtern bei Kindern und Erwachsenen: Die Rolle konzeptuellen Wissens. *Sprache und Kognition, 16*(1), 14-30.

Schwarzer, G. (2000). Development of face processing: The effect of face inversion. *Child Development, 71*(2), 391-401.

Schwarzer, G. & Korell, M. (2001). Gesichterverarbeitung im Kleinkind- und Vorschulalter. *Zeitschrift für Entwicklungs- und Pädagogische Psychologie, 33*(2), 78-90.

Seitz, K. (2002). Parts and wholes in person recognition: Developmental trends. *Journal of Experimental Child Psychology, 82*(4), 367-381.

Seitz, K. (in press). The effect of changes in posture and clothing on the development of unfamiliar person recognition. *Journal of Applied Cognitive Psychology*.

Seitz, K., Limmer R., & Schumann-Hengsteler, R. (September, 1999). *Aspects of person recognition: Preschoolers', schoolchildren's and adults' identification performance.* Poster presented at the 11. Conference of the European Society of Cognitive Psychology, Gent, Belgium.

Seitz, K., & Schumann-Hengsteler, R. (April, 1999). *Developmental trends in person recognition.* Poster presented at the Biennial Meeting of the Society for Research in Child Development, Albuquerque, NM.

Soppe, H. J. G. (1986). Children's recognition of unfamiliar faces: Developments and determinants. *International Journal of Behavioral Development, 9*, 219-233.

Tanaka, J. W., & Farah, M. J. (1993). Parts and wholes in face recognition. *The Quaterly Journal of Experimental Psychology, 46A*(2), 225-245.

Tanaka, J. W., Kay, B. K., Grinnell, E., Stansfield, B., & Szechter, L. (1998). Face recognition in young children: When the whole is greater than the sum of its parts. *Visual Cognition, 5*(4), 479-496.

Thomson, D. M., Robertson, S. L., & Vogt, R. (1982). Person recognition: The effect of context. *Human Learning, 1*, 137-154.

Yarmey, A. D. (1988). Streetproofing and bystander's memory for a child abduction. In M. Gruneberg, P. E. Morris, & M. Sykes (Eds.), *Practical aspects of memory*, (Vol. 1, pp.112-116). Chichester, UK: Wiley.

Address for Correspondence

Katja Seitz
Catholic University of Eichstätt-Ingolstadt
Ostenstr. 26-28
D-85072 Eichstätt
Germany
E-mail: katja.seitz@ku-eichstaett.de

Remembering Faces in Social Contexts

Claudia M. Roebers

9.1 Introduction

Remembering faces is of practical importance for our daily lives. The ability to recognize persons one has seen before, for example, may prevent embarrassment from not recognizing them later or from mistakenly taking a person for somebody else. This ability is also relevant in cases of eyewitness testimony where besides having to describe what happened, a witness may also be asked to identify a perpetrator of a crime. In these situations, incorrect identifications can have more serious consequences: Innocent people may be convicted, guilty people may be acquitted.

Given the importance of correct recognition of unfamiliar faces, it is not surprising that a large body of literature has addressed this issue. In this chapter, I will review the literature on identification accuracy from a developmental perspective, that is, discuss empirical findings on the ability of children to remember faces that were presented to them in a social context.

Whereas in real cases of testimony, witnesses are shown a line-up of real persons that contains the police suspect, empirical studies on identification accuracy use photos of faces for the identification task. An exception to this method is the study by Yarmey, Yarmey, and Yarmey (1996) who compared "live" identification procedures with photo identification procedures and found that the number of correct identifications did not differ between the two methods. Thus, it can be assumed that results obtained from photo identification procedures can be generalized to real cases of witnesses making an identification.

Empirical studies on identification accuracy can be classified either by the way the photo arrays are constructed or by the way the photos are presented to the witnesses. First, if a photo array contains the target person's photo that is to be recalled and identified, this is called a *target-present line-up*. If the target person's photo in the array has been replaced by a distractor photo and is therefore no longer part of the photo array, this is called a *target-absent line-up*. As will be described in more detail in the following paragraphs, the use of a target-absent or a target-present line-up generally results in very different findings, especially as far as developmental differences are concerned. A second way to classify studies on identification accuracy is the presentation mode: If all photos are presented at the same time to participants, this is called a *simultaneous presentation,* and has to be distinguished from studies in which the photos are presented sequentially to participants which is referred to as *sequential presentation*. In this type of presentation, the photos are shown one at a time to the participants who have to decide for every photo whether it is a target face or not. Since the use of target-present or target-absent line-ups and simultaneous or sequential presentation modes to study identification accuracy in children and adults strongly influences the pattern of results, especially developmental differences in identification accuracy, these procedures and their results will be reported separately.

9.2 Simultaneous Presentation of the Photos: Target-Present Line-Ups

An early study on identification abilities of children and adults in which a target-present line-up was used is reported by Marin, Holmes, Guth, and Kovac (1979). While 5-, 8-, and 11-year-olds as well as adults were interacting with the experimenter in a room, a confederate entered that room and argued with the experimenter about the use of the room, with the confederate being obviously annoyed. This disruption lasted for 15 seconds. Ten or 30 min later, participants were shown 6 photos simultaneously and asked to select the intruder. No developmental differences were observed with respect to the rates of correct identifications: 54% of the 5-year-olds, 45% of the 8-year-olds, 75% of the 11-year-olds, and 54% of the adults made a correct identification. Similarly, Goodman and Reed (1986) found no age-related increase in the ability to select a person's photo correctly when the face was present in the line-up. In their study, children and adults had interacted individually with the experimenter four to five days earlier. After delays of up to 9 days, even 5-year-old children demonstrated that they were as able as older children and adults to identify a person they had interacted with earlier correctly. This pattern of results for target-present line-ups was confirmed by Goodman, Hirschman, Hepps, and Rudy (1991) when the task was to identify a nurse who had taken a blood sample from the children.

Thus, from studies investigating children's identification abilities with the target present in the line-up, it appears that from the age of 5 or 6 years onwards, children and adults are equally able to make correct identifications of persons, whether they have only observed them briefly or interacted intensively with them earlier. Children younger than four years, however, appear to have poorer identification abilities, even in target-present line-ups (Goodman & Reed, 1986; Goodman et al., 1991; Pozzulo & Lindsay, 1998).

9.3 Simultaneous Presentation of Photos: Target-Absent Line-Ups

Different patterns of results concerning developmental differences in identification abilities are reported when the target face is not in the photo array, that is, when target-absent line-ups are used. Investigating individuals' tendency to select one photo in the absence of the target face can generally be considered as more ecologically valid, because in a real-life case of eyewitnesses giving identification evidence, the police has only a suspect. Naturally, in target-absent line-ups, the only appropriate reaction is not to choose any photo of the line-up, but instead answer with "I don't know" or "not present." In other words, whenever a selection is made from a target-absent line-up, it is a false identification (i.e., a false alarm).

Davies, Stevenson-Robb, and Flin (1988) had 7- to 12-year-old children interact with an experimenter in their schools who pretended to be giving a talk on appropriate behavior on the streets, and who asked small groups of 4 children to help him arrange chairs and equipment in preparation for his talk. Two weeks later, half of the children within each age group were assigned to the target-present and the other half to the target-absent line-up condition. The results showed, again, no age-related differences in correct identifications in the target-present line-up. However, in the target-absent line-up, 7- and 8-year-olds made significantly more false identifications than 9- to 12-year-olds.

These results have been confirmed by other studies, too, using different stimulus material such as slide shows about a picnic in a park with a thief appearing on the scene and stealing a radio. Even when participants are told that the target face of the thief might or might not be in the photo array, children show a stronger tendency to select a person in target-absent line-ups and thus make more errors than adults (Beal, Schmitt, & Dekle, 1995; Dekle, Beal, Elliott, & Honeycutt, 1996; Parker & Carranza, 1989; Parker & Ryan, 1993).

What are the reasons for the difficulty children have in rejecting a photo array when the target face is not present in the line-up? This question seems especially important because studies using target-present line-ups show that children aged 5 years and above are remarkably competent, and their high false alarm rates seem to be in contrast to what one would expect.

9.3.1 Demand Characteristics of the Identification Task

Davies (1993) argued that the higher rates of false identification in target-absent line-ups made by younger children in comparison to older children and adults is due to the demand characteristics of the identification task and the instructions given prior to the task. Younger children have repeatedly demonstrated a strong tendency to try and please the interviewer and fulfill the requirements of the task as well as they can. Their perception of the task demands, however, might be different from the perception of older children and adults and different from that of the interviewer (Poole & Lamb, 1998; Ornstein, 1995).

In order to avoid misperceptions such as these, Parker and Ryan (1993) trained 9-year-olds and adults before the critical identification task to reject a photo array if the target face was not present. In this training, a photo line-up was presented to the participants that either contained or did not contain the photo of the interviewer. Participants were asked to select the photo of the experimenter from the line-up and were also given feedback. Although the overall rate of false alarms was significantly reduced by prior training, the developmental differences favoring the adults remained. Other training studies have found similar results: Even though younger children can be trained to reject a photo array appropriately when the target face is absent, general age-related improvements in this ability cannot be totally eliminated by training (Goodman, Bottoms, Schwartz-Kenney, & Rudy, 1991). Methodological differences in the training itself do not seem to be the critical variable; Pozzulo and Lindsay (1998), for example, found that training can also be efficiently carried out with drawings of animals rather than with photos of people. Furthermore, more intense training does not result in a dramatic improvement of performance in children.

Another method to decrease the demand characteristics of the identification task and to reduce the tendency of children to select someone from the array when the target face is absent is to include a "Mr. Nobody" or "Not here" card in the photo array. In cases where the target person is not in the line-up, participants are instructed to select this card. In other words, with this procedure, participants always have to select a card, even if the target face is absent. There are two studies using this method to reduce guessing behavior in children and both attained similar results: Beal and colleagues (Beal et al., 1995) as well as Davies, Tarrant, and Flin (1989) achieved a significant increase in children's correct rejections of the target-absent photo array with the additional "Mr. Nobody" card compared to the usual target-absent line-up procedure. However, the improvement was not strong enough to increase young children's performance to the level of older children and adults. In sum, it can be assumed that the demand characteristics of the line-up identification task and children's inappropriate perception of these contribute significantly to the high rate of false alarms. Therefore, although children's performance can be improved, developmental differences remain (Pozzulo & Lindsay, 1998).

9.3.2 Exposure Time

Generally, it is assumed that the longer an individual looks at a face, the more likely he or she is to identify that face correctly later on. Goodman and Reed's (1986) study documents that, compared to older children and adults, younger children looked at people's faces for a shorter time. Interestingly, however, Gross and Hayne (1996) showed that it is the salience of a person and the person's behavior rather than the time of exposure that is critical for correct identification. In their study, 5- and 6-year-old children visited a fire station where they interacted with two confederates dressed up in fire fighter uniforms. There were two additional people they met and observed during their visit, a workman who was looking for his tool box and a woman who slid down the pole in front of the children. Although, in general, the rates of correct identification were higher for the two adults that were present the whole time during the trip, the "poleslider" was also correctly recognized by many children (65%). The salience of the woman's behavior, that is, sliding down the pole, must have contributed to the high percentage of correct identifications. Thus, it is not only the time of exposure that influences correct identification.

Similar results are reported by Roebers and Lockl (1999) who showed a short video about a conflict between two groups of children to 6- and 8-year-olds and adults. In this video, seven target faces are presented with different exposure times, that is, the length of time when only the target's face is zoomed into the film. There were no significant correlations between time of exposure and correct identification ($r = .15$). However, faces of those children who played a central role in the video were generally recognized better than faces of children who acted in minor roles. For example, the victim of the conflict and the gang leader were identified correctly by more than 90% of the participants, regardless of age.

A study by Beal and colleagues (Beal et al., 1995) also indicates that exposure time does not influence correct identification in children and adults substantially. In this study some of the 5-year-olds were shown a slide show twice about a picnic in the park and a woman appearing and stealing a camera. Despite the double exposure time, participants' rates of correct identification of the theft were not superior to the performance of participants who had watched the slide show only once.

9.3.3 Metacognitive Monitoring Processes

Another reason why young children show such a strong tendency to select any photo from an array even in the absence of the target face is their inability to monitor and control their recall efforts adequately. In general, these metacognitive monitoring and control processes develop relatively late in childhood and have been shown to influence the memory performance not only of children but also of adults significantly (Schneider, 1998). For example, young children have been shown to answer less often with "I don't know" and instead give more incorrect answers. This results in an overall impairment of recall accuracy in event recall tasks and in identification tasks compared to older children and adults (Beal et al., 1995; Cassel, Roebers, & Bjorklund, 1996; Roebers, Moga, & Schneider, 2001; Roebers &

Schneider, 2000). It appears that children have an inflated belief about their memory competence in general; in other words, children overestimate the confidence that their best-candidate answer is correct.

For adults, the appropriate evaluation of confidence that the selected face from the line-up is, in fact, the target person is associated positively with performance on an identification task. Lindsay and Wells (1985) reported an association between confidence and identification accuracy of r = .30. With regard to children, however, there are only two studies in which confidence judgments were included in the identification task. Parker and Ryan (1993) found that although children's and adults' levels of confidence did not differ significantly when collapsed across correct identifications and false alarms, when only false alarms were considered children's estimated confidence of having made a correct choice was significantly higher than that of adults.

In order to investigate children's biased evaluations of their confidence, Roebers and Lockl (1999) asked 6- and 8-year-olds as well as adults to rate their confidence on a 5-point scale for each of the presented faces (7 target faces from a video plus 14 distractor faces). The results showed that with increasing age, confidence judgments decreased, pointing to a growing ability to assess confidence adequately. Moreover, older children and adults proved to be better at distinguishing between correct identifications and false alarms in their confidence ratings, that is, appropriately giving higher confidence judgments after correct rather than incorrect selections. And, while for the 6-year-olds there was no significant association between metacognitive monitoring competency (i.e., the ability to differentiate appropriately between correct identifications and false alarms) and identification accuracy (hits and correct rejections), these two variables were correlated significantly and positively in the 8-year-old and adult groups. Those 8-year-olds and adults who were able to differentiate better between correct and incorrect answers in the identification task also showed higher identification accuracy (Roebers & Lockl, 1999) and this correlation increased with age.

In sum, children's poorer metacognitive monitoring skills, especially their over-optimistic evaluation of the accuracy of their choice in cases when they make an incorrect selection can be considered as one important factor influencing their identification performance. Because they have difficulty assessing that their answer might be wrong, their tendency to reject a target-absent line-up is low. It should be noted, however, that the ability of children to monitor and control their efforts to recall faces correctly does not necessarily mirror a global metacognitive deficit, but is a function of the demands of the recall situation. When the demand characteristics of the task are perceived more appropriately by children, they are able to perform adequate metacognitive monitoring processes and benefit from them in terms of recall performance. For example, if children are trained to use the "don't know" option (Goodman et al., 1991; Parker & Ryan, 1993), or are reminded that they can skip a question whenever they are unsure about the correct answer (Howie, 2002), or are highly motivated to give only correct answers (Roebers & Fernandez, in press; Roebers et al., 2001), children as young as 6 years of age can carry out efficient metacognitive monitoring.

9.4 Presentation Mode: Simultaneous Versus Sequential Line-Ups

As was outlined in the introduction, empirical studies investigating children and adults' identification accuracy can be classified by the way the photos of the faces are presented. Whereas in both target-absent and target-present line-ups all pictures are presented simultaneously, it is possible to present the photos (target faces and distractors) sequentially, that is, one at a time. The identification task then is to look at each photo carefully and indicate for every face whether it is a target face or not.

Lindsay and Wells (1985) have argued that the decision processes required during simultaneous versus sequential line-ups are qualitatively different in that the simultaneous presentation of target and distractor faces allows so called *relative judgments*. Relative judgments are characterized by the fact that individuals compare the photos of the array with their internal representation of the target face and select the photo that resembles it most. In contrast, when the photos are presented in a sequence, individuals have to decide for each photo in turn whether it is the target face or not. For this reason, the decision processes required in sequential line-ups are labeled *absolute judgments*. According to Lindsay and Wells (1985), when confronted with a line-up, a good strategy is to form relative judgments, but only if the target face is present. In fact, the high rates of false identifications in target-absent line-ups can be explained in part by erroneous relative judgments. They argue that individuals select the face from the line-up that resembles the target face most which, in target-absent line-ups, leads to a false choice. Supporting evidence for this assumption comes from studies with adults in which target-absent line-ups and sequential line-ups are compared. Lindsay and Wells (1985) showed that the number of false identifications was significantly smaller in sequential line-ups compared to target-absent line-ups, while, at the same time, the rate of correct identifications was not affected.

Developmental studies comparing simultaneous and sequential presentations of faces in identification tasks are rare. Parker and Ryan (1993) found that both children and adults made more correct rejections when the sequential presentation mode (54%) was used rather than the simultaneous presentation mode (29%). Similarly, Roebers and Lockl (1999) used a paradigm in which seven target faces were to be identified instead of the usual one or two. They report that with respect to false identifications (i.e., false alarms) there were no developmental differences for 6- and 8-year-olds and adults whether the simultaneous (target-present line-up) or the sequential presentation mode was used. With respect to correct identifications, there were developmental differences but these varied depending on whether the photos in the line-up had been presented simultaneously or sequentially. When the simultaneous presentation mode was used, 6-, 8-year-olds, and adults did not differ from each other, with hit rates being 80%, 79%, and 80% for the 6-, 8-year-olds, and adults, respectively. When the sequential presentation mode was used, however, hit rates of 6-year-olds (66%) were significantly lower than hit rates of 8-year-olds (80%) and adults (86%). Thus, Lindsay and Wells' (1985) assumptions that relative judgments facilitate the identification task by reducing the number of false alarms could largely be confirmed for children. However, contrary to what was found for adults, the rate of correct identifications seems to be affected negatively by the sequential presentation mode, at least for children younger than eight years.

9.4.1 Disadvantages of Sequential Line-Ups: The Problem of Multiple Selections

Despite the fact that the sequential presentation of photos seems to improve identification accuracy by reducing the likelihood of false alarms, another problem arises from this methodology. Since the photos are presented one at a time and the individual has to make an "on-line" decision as to whether or not the photo depicts a target face, the likelihood of multiple selections increases. In other words, individuals select more photos than target faces. Thus, the likelihood of a correct identification increases artificially, and if the number of false identifications is not taken into account, the results can be biased.

Developmental studies on face identification which have included measures of multiple selections have documented that children are especially prone to make this kind of error. Lindsay, Pozzulo, Craig, Lee, and Corber (1997) report, for example, that while only 5% of the adults made more selections than required, 74% of the children made multiple selections. Similar results with children making more selections are also described in Parker and Carranza (1989) and Parker and Ryan (1993).

In fact, a recent study using the same stimulus and identification material as Roebers and Lockl (1999) has shown that what, at first sight, is judged to be surprisingly good performance in the identification task by children younger than 8 years of age, can be assessed quite differently when multiple selections are considered. Roebers and Schneider (2001) investigated face recognition abilities of children aged 6, 8, and 10 years as well as adults. Participants were shown a video and asked to identify the seven target faces from the film three weeks later. The sequential line-up contained the 7 targets and 14 distractor photos. When the hit rates and false alarm rates were considered, Roebers and Schneider (2001) largely confirmed previous findings in that no significant age differences were found between 6-year-olds and adults. Overall, however, younger children made more false alarms. Moreover, when the number of selections made from the entire set of photos (21 photos) and the first third of the set (the first seven photos) is taken into account, children's "good" performance concerning the hit rates can be seen in a new light. Both for the entire set and for the first third, adults made significantly fewer selections (8.6 for the entire set) than all three groups of children who did not differ from each other (10.0, 11.2, 10.7, for the 6-, 8-, and 10-year-olds, respectively). Thus, children's high rates of correct identification are partly due to their stronger tendency to select a photo as being a target photo. By selecting more faces, children inflate the probability of a hit. Adults, on the other side, appeared to approach the task more appropriately by taking into account how many target faces were to be selected altogether and how many they had already selected. Their behavior clearly fulfilled the requirements of the identification task better.

9.5 Neutral Versus Social Contexts

Face recognition in children and adults is generally studied in two major, distinct areas of research: basic research on encoding strategies, and applied research of eyewitness memory which is mainly discussed in this chapter. Moreover, a study by Soppe (1986) which included a classical face recognition task and a typical eyewitness photo identification task for the same 8- to 13-year-olds found no significant correlation between the two measures of recognition performance, indicating that the underlying processes involved in these tasks are different.

In the following paragraphs, I will address differences in results emerging from these two lines of research and discuss reasons why the results and conclusions drawn from these two areas are so divergent. It should become clear that the encoding and retrieving processes differ substantially, and that, as a result, different encoding strategies and qualitatively different mental representations of the target faces emerge. However, as will also be outlined, there may be circumstances in an eyewitness identification task under which the encoding processes studied in basic research paradigms significantly influence accuracy of identification whatever the age of the eyewitness.

9.5.1 Differences in Methodology

In basic research on face recognition, participants are usually shown a large number of target photos of unknown persons in sequence, each photo being presented for 5 to 20 seconds. After a short delay of only a few minutes, they are instructed to indicate from a large number of photos (distractor (novel) faces and target faces) which are the targets. Performance is usually measured by the percentage of correct identifications (hits) and incorrect selections (false alarms), or by measures based on signal detection analyses (Carey, 1981). The results of this type of study generally show a steady improvement in the ability to recognize faces from the age of 5 onwards (Flin, 1980; for a review, see Davies, 1996).

The linear improvement in the ability of children to recognize faces seems surprising and discrepant considering the results emerging from applied studies. However, a number of important differences in the methods used to investigate how competent children are at identifying faces might account for children's good performance in eyewitness studies. In basic research on face processing, the use of multiple targets, static pictures during presentation, the concentration on faces, the cut-outs of body, clothes, movement and speech make the identification task, especially for children, much more difficult to accomplish than a task in which the target persons have been embedded in a complex social context, such as a slide show of a picnic with somebody sneaking up to steal something, a video about a conflict between two groups of children, or a personal interaction such as a nurse taking a blood sample (Davies, 1993).

Thus, methodological differences between basic research on face recognition and eyewitness identification contribute, at least to some extent, to the discrepant overall pattern of results.

9.5.2 A Theoretical Model for Face Recognition in Social Contexts

Bruce and Young (1986) as well as Bruce and Humphreys (1994) argued that, in eyewitness studies, factors of the social context cause faces to be encoded differently and this might have a positive influence on the number of faces recognized in social contexts. Moreover, the theoretical model outlined by Bruce and Young (1986) might explain the discrepant findings emerging from basic and applied research described in the previous paragraphs. The authors assume that different kinds of information can be extracted from faces. A pictorial code emerges when a static, visually presented pattern is looked at. A structural code is needed when the stimulus changes between encoding and testing, for example, when the angle is changed or when the hairstyle of a person is altered. Information about an unfamiliar person's age, character or assumed intelligence may be inferred from the social context during encoding and represented in the form of *visually derived semantic codes*. In contrast, the mental representation of a familiar face also contains social information such as the context in which this person is usually met, friends, profession etc. This fourth kind of information is stored in *identity-specific semantic codes*.

Besides these different kinds of information, it is assumed that individuals engage in different cognitive processes during encoding and retrieval depending on the characteristics of the facial stimuli. While a simple pictorial code is sufficient to recognize faces correctly when they are presented as static photos during the encoding and the retrieval phase, the recognition of faces that have been presented in a social context requires the activation of *face recognition units* that contain not only the visually derived semantic codes but also the identity-specific codes.

It is clear that Bruce and Young (1986) as well as Bruce and Humphreys (1994) assume that encoding and remembering faces that were presented as static pictures both during encoding and retrieval is a qualitatively different task than recognizing faces of persons who were involved in a complex social interaction. This additional information facilitates the identification task, especially for children. However, there may be certain circumstances in an eyewitness identification task when encoding processes or strategies being investigated in basic face recognition studies are triggered off. These encoding processes may then influence identification accuracy significantly. Although there is still not a great deal of empirical work bridging these two distinct areas of developmental research, the few existing studies will be described below.

9.5.3 Bridging the Gap Between two Research Fields

Wells and Hryciw (1984) proposed that the use of a retrieval task to recognize faces favors holistic encoding operations, as defined in basic research on face recognition. They argue that the relevant topographical cues of a face are preserved in the photos presented to participants in the recognition phase of the experiment. Consequently, when a holistic encoding strategy is used during the photo presentation of the line-up, it should facilitate correct recognition. The authors manipulated the encoding processes of the target and distractor faces during the identification task and found that those adults who used a holistic encoding strategy showed superior performance in face recognition.

Since children seem to have a stronger tendency to encode faces based on featural or configural information rather than holistically, children's performance during an identification task might be expected to be inferior to that of adults'. As Pozzulo and Lindsay (1998) have pointed out, gross discrimination based on single features such as hair color or shape (i.e., analytical processing; Schwarzer, 2000) may be sufficient to produce a correct identification in a target-present line-up. When the target is absent in the line-up, however, holistic processing may be necessary in order to reject the distractor faces. If children do not have access to or are not using holistic information to make identification decisions in target-absent line-ups, more incorrect identification decisions will be made compared to adults. Thus, differences between individuals in the way they process the photos presented during the identification task may account for differences in performance, at least to some extent.

Assuming that the underlying mechanisms are the same, more efficient encoding may also lead to poorer recognition in the presence of false information. To test this assumption, Roebers and Schneider (2001) carried out a typical misinformation paradigm adopted from Loftus (1979) consisting of an encoding phase of the event and faces to be recalled, an intermediate phase in which false information including static photos of distractor faces (misleading photos) were presented, and a final recognition test in which photos of the original faces, the misleading photos, and photos of new faces were used for a sequential line-up. Interestingly, while for measures of verbal recall, children's memory impairment was significantly larger than adults' memory impairment (due to the presentation of misleading information), adults made significantly more incorrect choices of photos used in the misleading phase than children. In contrast, there were no differences between the age groups in their tendency to mistake photos of new faces for the original faces. Roebers and Schneider (2001) interpreted this somewhat surprising result as showing that adults might have been more efficient in encoding the black and white static photos of the distractor faces than children which, in turn, led to an increase in the incorrect identification of these. Since more adults use a holistic encoding strategy to encode static presentations of faces compared to children, this may have led to the reversed age trend concerning the false alarms.

Importantly, not all children of one age group process faces analytically. In other words, there will always be some children of the same age who process faces holistically (Schwarzer, 2000). To find out whether children who encode faces holistically would show better performance in a face recognition test, Schwarzer and Roebers (2002) used the category learning task developed by Schwarzer (2000) that allows individual children (and adults) to be classified as using either a holistic or an analytical encoding strategy for faces. Based on the results of this category learning task, children using a holistic encoding strategy (20% of all children) were contrasted with the children who used an analytical encoding strategy (72%) in the face recognition test. The context in which the target faces were presented was manipulated so that half of the children of each age group were shown the target faces in a neutral context, i.e., they saw 7 slides of the target faces for 7 seconds each.

The other half of each age group was shown the target faces embedded in a complex social interaction, i.e., the video film was shown that had been used previously by Roebers and Lockl (1999) and Roebers and Schneider (2001). The results confirmed a significant influence of the social context, with children who had watched the video identifying more targets correctly than children who had only been shown the static photos. Interestingly, the tendency to select a distractor photo erroneously as a target face (false alarm) was not affected by the manipulation of the context during encoding.

When the relationship between recognition performance and encoding strategy was considered, it was found that a holistic encoding strategy was beneficial for recognition, but in the neutral context only (see also Chapter 4). In other words, when information of the social context was present, holistic and analytical encoding strategies did not lead to differences in later face recognition performance. However, when information about the social context was absent, a holistic strategy was associated with a larger mean number of correct identifications. It should be noted that a holistic or analytical encoding strategy did not affect the number of false alarms or the discrimination index as measures of overall identification accuracy (Schwarzer & Roebers, 2002).

9.5.4 Concluding Remarks

The aim of the present chapter was to provide an easy-to-understand overview of the literature on the development of face identification. Factors significantly influencing the ability of children to recognize a target face correctly, and differences in methodology between applied and basic research paradigms have been discussed. The limited research available has confirmed what was expected, namely that encoding strategies emphasizing overall similarity rather than taking single facial attributes into account lead to superior performance in face identification tasks. In other words, the preferred encoding strategy for faces can account for age-related differences as they are typically observed in face recognition studies. Importantly, however, this only seems to be the case in the absence of any information about the social context. When faces are encoded within a social context, encoding processes, the resulting mental representation, and retrieval of faces appear to be qualitatively different and are also responsible for different developmental growth functions.

Acknowledgements

The empirical research described in this chapter was financed by the German Research Foundation (Grant No. FOR 261/2-1) within the Research Group "Cognitive Development." I am grateful to Wolfgang Schneider for his continuous support and to all members of the Research Group for the fruitful discussions on the work carried out in cooperation with Gudrun Schwarzer.

References

Beal, C. R., Schmitt, K. L., & Dekle, D. J. (1995). Eyewitness identification of children: Effects of absolute judgments, nonverbal response options, and event encoding. *Law and Human Behavior, 19*, 197-217.

Bruce, V., & Humphreys, G. W. (1994). Recognizing objects and faces. In V. Bruce & G. W. Humphreys (Eds.), *Object and face recognition* (pp. 141-180). Hove, UK: Laurence Erlbaum.

Bruce, V., & Young, A. (1986). Understanding face recognition. *British Journal of Psychology, 77*, 305-327.

Carey, S. (1981). The development of face perception. In G. Davies, H. Ellis & J. Shepherd (Eds.), *Perceiving and remembering faces* (pp. 9-34). London: Academic Press.

Cassel, W. S., Roebers, C. M., & Bjorklund, D. F. (1996). Developmental patterns of eyewitness responses to repeated and increasingly suggestive questions. *Journal of Experimental Child Psychology, 61*, 116-133.

Davies, G. M. (1993). Children's memory for other people: An integrative review. In K. Nelson (Ed.), *Memory and affect in development (Vol.26 of the Minnesota Symposia on Child Psychology)* (pp. 123-157). Hillsdale, NJ: Laurence Erlbaum Ass.

Davies, G. M. (1996). Children's identification evidence. In S. L. Sporer, R. S. Malpass & G. Köhnken (Eds.), *Psychological issues in eyewitness identification* (pp. 233-258). Hillsdale, NJ: Laurence Erlbaum Ass.

Davies, G. M., Stevenson-Robb, Y., & Flin, R. (1988). Tales out of school: Children's memory for an unexpected incident. In M. Gruneberg, P. Morris & R. Sykes (Eds.), *Practical aspects of memory* (Vol. 1, pp. 122-127). Chicester, UK: Wiley.

Davies, G. M., Tarrant, A., & Flin, R. (1989). Close encounters of the witness kind: Children's memory for a simulated health inspection. *British Journal of Psychology, 80*, 415-429.

Dekle, D. J., Beal, C. R., Elliott, R., & Honeycutt, D. (1996). Children as witnesses: A comparison of lineup versus show-up identification methods. *Applied Cognitive Psychology, 10*, 1-12.

Flin, R. H. (1980). Age effects in children's memory for unfamiliar faces. *Developmental Psychology, 16*, 373-374.

Goodman, G. S., Bottoms, B., Schwartz-Kenney, B. M., & Rudy, L. (1991). Children's memory for a stressful event: Improving children's reports. *Journal of Narrative and Life History, 1*, 69-99.

Goodman, G. S., Hirschman, J. E., Hepps, D., & Rudy, L. (1991). Children's memory for stressful events. *Merrill-Palmer Quarterly, 37*, 109-149.

Goodman, G. S., & Reed, R. S. (1986). Age differences in eyewitness testimony. *Law and Human Behavior, 10*, 317-332.

Gross, J., & Hayne, H. (1996). Eyewitness identification by 5- to 6-year-old children. *Law and Human Behavior, 20*, 359-373.

Howie, P. (2002). Answering the unanswerable: Appropriate "don't know" responding in children's event reporting. *Paper submitted for publication.*

Lindsay, R. C. L., Pozzulo, J. D., Craig, W., Lee, K., & Corber, S. (1997). Simultaneous lineups, sequential lineups, and show-ups: Eyewitness identification decisions of adults and children. *Law and Human Behavior, 21*, 391-404.

Lindsay, R. C. L., & Wells, G. L. (1985). Improving eyewitness identifications from lineups: Simultaneous versus sequential lineup presentation. *Journal of Applied Psychology, 70*, 556-564.

Loftus, E. F. (1979). *Eyewitness Testimony.* Cambridge, MA: Harvard University Press.

Marin, B. V., Holmes, D. L., Guth, M., & Kovac, P. (1979). The potential of children as eyewitnesses. *Law and Human Behavior, 3*, 295-306.

Ornstein, P. A. (1995). Children's long-term retention of salient personal experiences. *Journal of Traumatic Stress, 8,* 581-604.

Parker, J. F., & Carranza, L. E. (1989). Eyewitness testimony of children in target-present and target-absent lineups. *Law and Human Behavior, 13,* 133-149.

Parker, J. F., & Ryan, V. (1993). An attempt to reduce guessing behavior in children's and adults' eyewitness identifications. *Law and Human Behavior, 17,* 11-26.

Poole, D. A., & Lamb, M. E. (1998). *Investigative interviews of children: A guide for helping professionals.* Washington, DC: American Psychological Association.

Pozzulo, J. D., & Lindsay, R. C. L. (1998). Identification accuracy of children and adults: A meta-analysis. *Law and Human Behavior, 22,* 549-570.

Roebers, C. M., & Fernandez, O. (in press). The effects of accuracy motivation on children's and adults' event recall, suggestibility, and their answers to unanswerable questions. *Journal of Cognition and Development.*

Roebers, C. M., & Lockl, K. (1999). Der Einfluß von Metakognitionen und vorheriger Irreführung auf die Identifikationsleistungen kindlicher Augenzeugen. *Zeitschrift für Entwicklungspsychologie und Pädagogische Psychologie, 31,* 116-126.

Roebers, C. M., Moga, N., & Schneider, W. (2001). The role of accuracy motivation on children's and adults event recall. *Journal of Experimental Child Psychology, 78,* 313-329.

Roebers, C. M., & Schneider, W. (2000). The impact of misleading questions on eyewitness memory in children and adults. *Applied Cognitive Psychology, 14,* 509-526.

Roebers, C. M., & Schneider, W. (2001). Memory for an observed event in the presence of prior misinformation: Developmental patterns in free recall and identification accuracy. *British Journal of Developmental Psychology, 19,* 507-524.

Schneider, W. (1998). The development of procedural metamemory in childhood and adolescence. In G. Mazzoni & T. O. Nelson (Eds.), *Metacognitive and cognitive neuropsychology: Monitoring and control processes* (pp. 1-21). Mahwah, NJ: L. Erlbaum.

Schwarzer, G. (2000). Development of face processing: The effect of face inversion. *Child Development, 71,* 391-401.

Schwarzer, G., & Roebers, C. M. (2002). Children's face recognition in different contexts: The role of encoding strategies. *Perceptual and Motor Skills, 94,* 281-294.

Soppe, H. J. G. (1986). Children's recognition of unfamiliar faces: Developments and determinants. *International Journal of Behavioral Development, 9,* 219-233.

Wells, G. L., & Hryciw, B. (1984). Memory for faces: Encoding and retrieval operations. *Memory & Cognition, 12,* 338-344.

Yarmey, A. D., Yarmey, M. J., & Yarmey, A. L. (1996). Accuracy of eyewitness identification in show-ups and lineups. *Law and Human Behavior, 20,* 459-447.

Address for Correspondence

Claudia M. Roebers
University of Würzburg
Department of Psychology IV
Röntgenring 10
D-97070 Würzburg
Germany
E-mail: roebers@psychologie.uni-wuerzburg.de